ALA Studies in Librarianship, 11

Subject Control of Film and Video

A COMPARISON OF THREE METHODS

Lucienne Maillet

American Library Association
Chicago and London, 1991

Designed by Charles Bozett

Composed by Point West, Inc.,
in Bodoni text with Eras display
on a Compugraphic Quadex 5000 and
output on a Compugraphic 9600 laser
typesetter

Printed on 50-pound Glatfelter, a pH neutral
stock, and bound in 10-point Carolina
cover stock by Braun-Brumfield, Inc.

The paper used in this publication meets the minimum requirements of American National Standard for Information Sciences—Permanence of Paper for Printed Library Materials, ANSI Z39.48-1984. ∞

Library of Congress Cataloging-in-Publication Data

Maillet, Lucienne G.
    Subject control of film and video : a comparison of three methods / by Lucienne Maillet.
    p. cm. — (ALA studies in librarianship ; no. 11)
    Includes bibliographical references.
    ISBN 0-8389-0553-6 (alk. paper)
    1. Cataloging of motion pictures. 2. Cataloging of video recordings. 3. Subject headings—Motion pictures—Evaluation. 4. Subject headings—Video recordings—Motion pictures—Evaluation. 5. Motion pictures—Abstracting and indexing. 6. Video recordings—Abstracting and indexing. 7. Subject cataloging. I. Title. II. Series: ALA studies in librarianship : no. 11.
Z695.64.M35 1991
025.3'473—dc20   90-45127
                                CIP

Copyright © 1991 by the American Library Association. All rights reserved except those which may be granted by Sections 107 and 108 of the Copyright Revision Act of 1976.

Printed in the United States of America.

95 94 93 92 91   5 4 3 2 1

In memory of
Jane E. Stevens,
my mentor and my friend.

Contents

    Introduction   vii

1   Bibliographic Control of Film and Video   1

    Government   2
    The Nonprofit Sector   8
    The Private Sector   11
    Partnership   17
    Summary   22

2   Access to Film and Video   25

    Bibliographic Standards   27
    Subject Access   28
    Methodology of Study   34
        Vocabulary   37
        Content Description   39
        Structure of Headings   40
        Strengths and Weaknesses   41

3   Library of Congress Subject Headings   43

    Background   43
    Organization of LCSH   48
    Analysis of the LC Index   52
    Strengths and Weaknesses   59

4   National Information Center for Educational Media   64

    Background   64
    Organization of the NICEM Index   67
    Analysis of Index   69
    Strengths and Weaknesses   75

5   Preserved Context Index System   79

       Background   79
       Organization of PRECIS   83
       Analysis of Index   94
       Strengths and Weaknesses   102

6   Alternatives in Subject Access   106

       Media Collections   106
       Access   107
       Subject Access   108
       Exhaustivity of Indexing   112

       Appendix: A Sample PRECIS Index   117

       Bibliography   141

Introduction

My involvement with films goes back a long way. I have fond childhood memories of my family's weekly ritual of moviegoing. In school, I eagerly anticipated the occasional film that was intended as enrichment to my education. During the 1960s, I handled films first as a high school science teacher and later as an elementary school librarian in the Montgomery County Public School System in Maryland, one of the most progressive school systems in the country at the time. One hundred seven schools in that system had intellectual access to the system's centralized film collection through each school's library card catalog. In spite of Montgomery County's systematic organization of its collection, accessible through a card catalog in each school, I was often dissatisfied when I searched for films by subject. Some of the films did not meet my needs because of the way they had been described; others came to my attention purely by accident. Colleagues shared my dissatisfaction. Clearly, more and better subject information was needed.

In 1970, I became head of Audiovisual Services at York College of the City University of New York. Among my responsibilites were the development of a film collection and the rental of films for classroom use. Teachers frequently asked for assistance in selecting films by subject. Films with known titles and producers were more easily researched in existing bibliographic tools. Identifying films on specific subjects was not so easy, for subject access to educational films remained a problem. While marketing the film *Focus on French*, produced by my husband, Daniel, in 1970, I found that the subject headings assigned for the film were too "book-oriented" and inadequate to do justice to the content and the approach to the subject. Since others have been equally critical of existing systems for accessing media, "home-grown" subject indexes for many film collections have been adopted to overcome the limitations of the existing subject access systems and the lack of standardized terminology in describing media.

Video first appeared in my own home in the early 1950s. However, my library's first contact with the medium came in 1970, when we purchased equipment to videotape campus programs. We transferred instructional films to videotape for convenience in use. Later, we purchased videocassettes for our collection. This format requires the same type of bibliographic control as motion pictures.

Later, as a teacher of cataloging at the Palmer School of Library and Information Science of Long Island University, I gained greater insight into subject cataloging of audiovisual materials. I came to realize that the complexity of the process is not a justification for its limitations on subject access.

All of us are familiar with the phrase, "A picture is worth a thousand words," which has served to remind us that visual images convey meaning with ease when we may have difficulty using words to describe visual images or create a surrogate description. Visual images have ranged from the concrete—a picture of a personal experience—to the abstract—a pictorial representation captured on film. Subject access systems for media have had to describe and interpret not only visual images but also the effect of sound and motion on that message. Simply adopting cataloging practices for print has not adequately reflected the complexity of the task. The assignment of a limited number of subject headings has often meant that much of film's content has not been available for retrieval, nor do these subject headings provide an analysis and interpretation of the visual and aural images.

Potential users have often had to rely heavily on annotations produced by marketing staffs to obtain a detailed description of individual films or video. The needs of users may not have been met, and yet catalogers have not been put to task to ameliorate the situation. It is the responsibility of the library profession to continue to explore new subject approaches and to identify ways to apply technology to improve the subject access to specialized and valuable film and video resources.

In 1978, PRECIS came to my attention. PREserved Context Index System (PRECIS) was a new indexing system being used by the British Library. It was being acclaimed as a serious rival to traditional subject heading systems. I was eager to learn about the new system; therefore, I enrolled in a seminar taught by its British founder, Derek Austin, at the University of Maryland.

A year later, this general indexing system was applied to films. The National Film Board of Canada produced a PRECIS index to its 1979 Atlantic regional catalog and subsequently adopted the system for all of its media catalogs, both manual and online. In the United States, media specialist Mary Sive generated an experimental PRECIS index for the

American Film Festival catalog of the Educational Film Library Association (EFLA), currently known as the American Film and Video Association (AFVA). Is PRECIS the long-awaited solution to the problems encountered in the subject cataloging of films and video? Does the PRECIS indexing provide comprehensive treatment of both topical and nontopical aspects of media? Are there significant differences between PRECIS indexing for film and video with subject access provided by the Library of Congress (LC) or the National Information Center for Educational Media (NICEM)?

The only way to answer these questions and more would be to study this new system and compare it to the other subject access systems currently being used to describe films and video. What began as a mild professional curiosity evolved into doctoral research and this book.

I analyzed the headings assigned to one hundred educational films under three different systems: (1) PRECIS, (2) the *Library of Congress Subject Headings*, eighth edition and supplements (1975–78), and (3) the subject index to *The NICEM Index to 16mm Educational Films*, seventh edition (1980). I studied the philosophy of access of each system, analyzed the structure, and identified the strengths and weaknesses of each system.

The Library of Congress applied its subject headings to films in 1951; the NICEM and PRECIS subject approaches to media are much more recent in origin. NICEM indexing first appeared in the early 1960s, and PRECIS in the mid 1970s. It may be argued that it is unfair to judge a system or an approach by criteria that did not exist when it was designed. However, this argument does not stand up to close scrutiny. Subject access systems are mechanisms devised to carry out particular tasks in the organization of all types of materials. They should be judged in light of how well they continue to perform their assigned tasks in manual catalogs and, more important, how well they respond to the rigorous demands of online retrieval.

I hope this analysis will be useful to librarians, media specialists, teachers, and users of film and video collections. My analysis is based on the assumption that more effective utilization of the existing subject access systems can be gained through a better understanding of their application to films and video. It gives guidance in the selection of a subject access system to those developing media catalogs. It offers suggestions for better ways to modify or enhance existing systems that provide subject access to films and video programs.

I wish to extend special thanks to the following people who have given me guidance and encouragement during the preparation of this manuscript:

Katherine Oliva, editor, Grumman Corporation, for helping me transform a dissertation into a book.

Herbert Bloom, senior editor, ALA Books, for reading the manuscript for its overall clarity.

The staff of Academic Computing of Long Island University for assistance in computerization of the manuscript.

Remaining errors, omissions, and ambiguities are entirely my responsibility.

CHAPTER

1
Bibliographic Control of Film and Video

Some types of information are best conveyed through visualization, particularly the moving image, which is a potent medium of communication in both film and video formats. The camera's eye is able to interpret a subject in a number of different ways. According to George Rehrauer of the Graduate School of Library Service, Rutgers University, it is also unique.

> Film has all the characteristics of language.... Broken lines can be used to convey a sense of disorganization or unrest; spirituality can be expressed by vertical lines, while rest and ease are sometimes implied by horizontal lines.... [Lighting] is used to create moods, to give feeling of depth, and to make the image aesthetically pleasing.... Another unique quality of film is its ability to compress, expand, or exaggerate time.[1]

The varied styles of presentation possible with motion pictures in film or video formats appeal to a diverse audience. The film scholar concentrates on the literary value of film, while the movie buff is more interested in how technique conveys a message. Entertainment is the only objective of some videocassette users, while educators frequently use films or video to aid them in describing concepts at specific grade levels in their subject areas.

The film medium was gradually accepted as a source of invaluable records of the past and present, even though the rate of film production has increased slowly but steadily. In contrast, video was accepted virtually overnight, and the medium has almost become a consumable item. However, the potential impact of these media is dependent on the intellectual access to specific items through the indexing system adopted. The handling of video in libraries has simulated the bestseller phenomenon—heavy circulation of popular titles with limited cataloging at best. Unfortunately, there has been insufficient concern for the bibliographic control of either format in selection tools, acquisition procedures, or subject and descriptive cataloging and classification.

This chapter will trace the history of the physical and bibliographic control of moving image media by the U.S. government and by both the nonprofit and private sectors. A review of resource lists will not only identify gaps in media coverage but will also focus on the deficiencies in their subject access methodology.

In 1969, the United States Office of Education organized a media institute, Systems and Standards for the Bibliographic Control of Media, to survey the situation and to elicit recommendations for solving the problem of bibliographic control. Forty-nine specialists in the organization and use of media concluded that nonprint media was not organized for intelligent selection and utilization:

> professional bibliographers in the Association for Educational Communications and Technology, the Educational Film Library Association, the American Society of Information Science and the American Library Association have failed to establish standards, while commercial companies less constrained by tradition are answering the cries of collectors and users with incompatible schemes, codes, and forms of bibliographic entry.[2]

The concerns expressed did not mean that there had been a total disregard for the bibliographic control of media.

Various groups have been involved with the control of newer media over the years. Their efforts have been traced to determine their contributions before and after the media institute. Through agencies like the Library of Congress (LC), the U.S. government has contributed significantly to the descriptive and subject cataloging of the two media. Commercial firms have also advanced the intellectual access to nonprint through their marketing catalogs, especially when bibliographic tools were nonexistent. Some firms have generated bibliographic indexes to nonprint; others have provided reviews and review indexes. In the nonprofit sector, universities, public and school libraries, museums, and professional associations have played a major role in standardizing subject access to films and video through their catalogs.

GOVERNMENT

Overview

Through the years, the government has assumed a leading role in the physical and bibliographic control of media. The U.S. government has fostered the development of standards for the descriptive and subject cataloging of nonprint for both manual and online catalogs. MARC records in print and online have been incorporated in many media catalogs in this country and abroad. In addition to being the largest producer and distributor of films and video, the U.S. government has provided financial support for media projects such as NICEM and Project MEDIA BASE and through the sponsorship of institutes has also encouraged a dialogue among members of the various professions mutually concerned with the control and use of media.

The federal government has also provided financial assistance to many worthwhile projects relating to the production of video materials. In 1960, it helped to setup the Great Plains National Instructional Library to circulate television courses on videotape among interested schools. The Agency for Instructional Television also received government funds to strengthen education through video.

Film records with LC subject headings have been included in the catalogs of libraries and in the databases of the major bibliographic utilities including OCLC, Research Library Information Network, and Western Library Network. Through these utilities, libraries have joined the Library of Congress in the cataloging of films and video by generating the records directly into their databases.

Over the years, the U.S. government has also provided some control of films and video by including titles of the works in catalogs produced by various governmental agencies, such as the U.S. Department of Health, Education, and Welfare's *U.S. Government Films for Public Educational Use—1963*, which included only broad subject categories linking the films by subject. There had been no central clearinghouse of government-produced media until 1968, when the National Audiovisual Center began to list thousands of titles produced over the years by the federal government in its catalog, *United States Government Films; A Catalog of Motion Pictures and Filmstrips for Sale by the National Audiovisual Center*. By the mid 1960s, many of the films were available on video. In 1974, the National Audiovisual Center renamed its catalog because it now listed materials in different formats. *The Catalog of United States Government Produced Audiovisual Materials* listed over 4,000 titles including films, video, and slide sets.

History of Physical and Bibliographic Control

Paper prints of early films were copyrighted as photographs, because, until 1912, there was no provision in the U.S. copyright law for the registration of "moving" pictures. Between 1894 and 1912, approximately 3,000 films were registered as photographs and recorded in the Copyright Office's *Catalogue of Copyright Entries*. The first catalog to include films, it contained the most complete record of films produced in the Untied States during the first half of the twentieth century. Fortunately, the paper prints were preserved by LC's Division of Prints, which was established in 1897. In 1967, Kemp Niver described the early films in detail in the *Library of Congress Paper Print Collection, 1894–1912*, a publication of the University of California Press.

The Townsend Act of 1912 provided for the copyright of films by requiring that a copy of the film be deposited with the Library of Congress. However, due to their flammable nature, nitrate films were returned to the producers, and LC retained substitutes for the films, such as posters and shooting scripts.

Meanwhile, the government recognized the value of training with films. In 1912, films produced by the U.S. Department of Agriculture were given to land-grant colleges. The film depository collections that resulted became the first educational film collections in the United States. By 1919, the U.S. Bureau of Educational Motion Pictures was distributing war films to extension divisions of colleges and universities, state departments of education, normal schools, and museums. By the mid-1940s, the U.S. government had become the largest producer, distributor, and user of films.

In 1934, the National Archives recognized the unique value of the motion picture camera for recording historical events and set up a Motion Picture and Sound Recording Division.

The Library of Congress also became involved in the physical control of films produced in the United States. A separate motion picture section was set up in the Library of Congress in 1943 to convert paper prints to safety film, acquire through private donations films not retained by LC during 1912 to 1942 and collect post-1942 films recommended by the Museum of Modern Art. The Library of Congress has maintained a shelflist of the safety films. The collection includes all the American Film Institute films that were converted to acetate. However, this file has been accessible only by title. In the 1980s, the Library of Congress through its optical disc program, experimented with the preservation of film memorabilia and produced a still-image videodisc of 90,000 motion picture publicity stills from the Motion Picture, Broadcasting and Recorded Sound Division. The stills were filmed in 35mm color film and transferred to videotape, which was used to produce a master videodisc.

Bibliographic Control

With an increasing number of films being produced, more complete bibliographic information was needed. Starting in 1946, the film records in the United States government's *Catalog of Copyright Entries* were expanded. No longer would the records serve solely as legal records; they would also provide standard bibliographic information to meet the steadily increasing needs of film buffs and scholars. Cataloging rules for film were drafted for the first time in the Copyright Office. Each entry in the catalog included credits, names of cast members, and a brief synopsis of the film's content. These amplified records, which were derived from actual viewing of the films, were contained in a new and totally separate publication entitled *Catalog of Copyright Entries: Motion Pictures and Filmstrips.*

The new film catalog enjoyed unprecedented sales, and the interest of the film community prompted the Library of Congress to investigate producing printed cards for film similar to those it produced for books. In 1951, with the encouragement of the library community, the film cataloging rules of the Copyright Office were modified by LC so that its printed card program could be extended to films. The library also decided to provide subject access to films through the *Library of Congress Subject Headings.* According to Katherine Clugston, head of the Audiovisual Section at LC in 1971, "When our film card program was initiated in 1952, people did not want Library of Congress subject headings on Library of Congress cards for films."[3]

Despite opposition, however, the library's catalogers assigned the same subject headings that had been created for books on the subject. Clugston explained why LC decided to use its own subject heading list for films instead of the *Sears List of Subject Headings,* widely used in schools and public libraries:

> However we were geared to give the LC subject headings and no other, and that was all we could do. Therefore, we settled for LC subject headings when we started.[4]

Clugston also indicated, however, that users did not like the LC headings for films because they were "too specific and too complicated." She later addressed those criticisms by making suggestions to the audiovisual community for consideration:

> We cannot change our subject heading list, but we are willing to consider the addition of curriculum-oriented subject topics, if a definite list can be prepared and accepted by the various educational and audiovisual groups that are concerned with the utilization of films.[5]

However, no action was ever taken by LC or the audiovisual community to add curricular headings for educational films.

Copyrighted films continued to be cataloged by the U.S. Copyright Office, while uncopyrighted films were cataloged by LC. The information supplied by producers and distributors was used by LC for cataloging films because catalogers did not have the equipment or the time required to preview them. Films were then assigned LC subject headings based on marketing information. From 1951 to 1957, catalog cards were available for virtually all copyrighted films and for a large number of other films for which some information was available from a secondary source. This joint effort between the Copyright Office and the Library of Congress facilitated a major advance toward national bibliographic control of films by centralizing the available information.

In 1958, the Copyright Office discontinued the cataloging of films and the Library of Congress assumed responsibility for all film cataloging. The increased workload, however, resulted in a decision to catalog only the copyrighted items added to LC's collection. This constituted a serious setback for the movement toward the bibliographic control of film.

Sumner Spalding, assistant director, Cataloging and Processing Department, Library of Congress, explained the position of the library thus:

> We concluded that we would not be able to function effectively in the field of the newer media developed primarily for younger students and because we do not collect them, we are not familiar with them and therefore, we do not have the expertise required for their effective organization. Some of the audiovisual media are of broad interest to general libraries as well as to school media centers, and in this area we do have a competence. I think that it is not going to be possible for you to look to the Library of Congress for coverage.[6]

Nevertheless, traditional libraries integrated the LC printed cards for films into their LC-based card catalogs, and the *Library of Congress Subject Headings* (LCSH) became the main subject access system for media by default.

The issuance of printed cards for films cataloged by the Library of Congress meant that film records would appear in the *National Union Catalog* (NUC). A separate volume for motion pictures and filmstrips was published as part of the *Library of Congress Author Catalog, 1948–1952*. This NUC volume represented the first attempt by LC to develop a national film bibliography. Films cataloged between 1952 and 1982 were included in the quarterly, annual, and quinquennial issues of NUC under the title *Library of Congress Catalogs: Audiovisual Materials*. Since 1983, the Library of Congress has published only a microfiche edition of the *National Union Catalog: Audiovisual Materials*, which features full record registers and separate indexes for names, titles, subjects, and series. These catalogs have provided subject access to film and video through the headings cumulated in the *Library of Congress Subject Headings*, now in its eleventh edition.

In the 1960s, television news was recognized as worthy of collecting and indexing. But it was not until ten years later that the National Archives and Records Service started to collect television network news in coordination with the three major networks. *The U.S. Catalog: Motion Pictures* was produced by the Audiovisual and Archives Division of the National Archives to provide subject access to the news collection.

When the Copyright Revision Act of 1976 assured the legality of television news, Congress mandated the establishment of the American Television and Radio Archives under the auspices of the Motion Picture, Broadcasting, and Sound Recordings Division of LC.

In 1966, the Library of Congress designed the Machine-Readable Cataloging (MARC) communications format to store cataloging data in a central source and to use the machine-readable records to produce various products, such as catalog cards, book catalogs, and bibliographies.

Since data in a machine record consists of a continuous stream of characters, the different parts of a bibliographic record have had to be explicitly identified for machine manipulation into separate fields. The fields in a record are coded to facilitate the retrieval of the component parts of each field. Bibliographic records using the MARC format include fields which contain subject or subject-rich information. The following variable fields in the 600 series, which store subject-added entries, are the primary sources of subject information:

TAG	FIELD
600	Personal name
610	Corporate name
611	Conference or meeting name
630	Uniform title
650	Topical
651	Geographic
652	Reversed geographic
653	Uncontrolled heading
654	Genre heading

The fields 650–655 generally contain the assigned Library of Congress subject headings. The variable fields 690–695 in the MARC records are reserved for local subject headings.

In 1970, LC developed a MARC format for films, *Films, a MARC Format,* which was renamed the *Visual Materials Format* in 1983 to extend the coverage to all two-dimensional materials.

By about this same time, the Library of Congress made limited progress in the bibliographic control of films produced in the United States. Meanwhile, Donald Beckwith and Allen Mirwis of Indiana University had analyzed film titles from major and minor sources of information about films and from the catalogs of approximately 200 film libraries. They developed a core list of films and found that the LC catalogs provided a more comprehensive listing of film information for the sample than any other current bibliographic tool.[7] Yet only 40 percent of the titles from the sample were identified in LC catalogs.

With the expansion of the audiovisual media in the United States, the government expressed concern for the bibliographic control of nonprint by sponsoring research on the subject. In 1976, the National Commission on Libraries and Information Science (NCLIS) set up a task force called Project MEDIA BASE to survey the cataloging practices of institutions with large media collections. The task force found such a disparity in cataloging practices that they recommended the development of a national bibliographic database for audiovisual resources. Unfortunately, this project was never realized.

Another government agency, the National Library of Medicine, has kept track of medical films in its MEDLINE database. By 1976, its online list, known as Audiovisuals Online, included 3,000 items and was growing at the rate of 200 items a month. The Medical Subject Headings have provided access to specialized media. Subject access to all materials including films in the MEDLINE database was provided through Medical Subject Headings (MeSH), a technical controlled vocabulary.

By the mid-1980s, LC's cataloging of audiovisual materials had become more comprehensive because LC attempted to catalog all audiovisual materials released in the United States and Canada that had educational or instructional value. The bibliographic information for films included in NUC by the Library of Congress has been supplied mainly by producers, distributors, and film libraries. LC currently obtains cooperative cataloging from approximately 1,100 U.S. and Canadian libraries. In most cases, cataloging is still done from accompanying materials, not from viewing the film or video.

THE NONPROFIT SECTOR

Many states have used the MARC data elements to describe their print and nonprint collections in the development of regional or state databases.

OCLC Online Computer Library Center

An Ohio database was created in 1967 by the Ohio College Library Center. Its purpose was to provide online shared cataloging for the academic libraries of Ohio. Libraries throughout the United States were subsequently allowed to participate in this bibliographic utility through regional networks like SOLINET. When cataloging records were not found in the OCLC database by participating libraries, they were encouraged to input their original cataloging into the database. In 1978, the utility name was changed to OCLC, Inc., to reflect its growing national orientation. Now named OCLC Online Computer Library Center Inc., it is commonly still referred by the acronym.

The OCLC Online Union Catalog (OLUC) contained 21 million records with supporting indexes, as of January 1990.[8] It is accessed by more than 10,000 participating institutions from 37 countries, including academic, public, federal, medical, and corporate libraries. At the present time, a million items are cataloged by participants every five to seven months. OLUC also contains records from special programs, including Cooperative Online Serials (CONSER), the U.S. Newspaper Program, and Major Microforms Program. There are approximately half a million audiovisual records in the OCLC database.

The following subject authorities were adopted by OCLC for subject headings in the records: LC Subject Headings, LC Subject Headings for Children's Literature (known as the Annotated Card Program), the National Library of Medicine Subject Headings (MeSH), the National Agricultural Library Subject Headings, the National Library of Canada Subject Headings, *Sears List of Subject Headings,* and local headings.

However, the OCLC computer program was not originally designed for subject retrieval. OCLC began to offer subject access to its computerized records in January 1990, after a reconfiguration of its computer system. Its EPIC program permits subject browsing and searching of the database and features keyword and phrase searching as well as the use of Boolean and adjacency operators. Twenty-two indexes were created from records to expand the searching capabilities of the system.

Meanwhile, a million citations in eight formats from OLUC were reformatted into the Electronic Access to Subject Information (EASI) reference database of another bibliographic utility, Bibliographic Retrieval Service (BRS). Since 1980, this utility has applied its subject access capability to a subset of OLUC. This database contains records with input dates spanning the most recent four-year period and represents recently published items acquired and cataloged by OCLC participants. It is updated quarterly to reflect the activity of OLUC and is reloaded each year to eliminate duplicate records, delete old records, and add new records. The search options in the BRS retrieval system permit access to keyword and phrase searching of controlled vocabulary. Free-text searching of words within the headings and of corporate or conference names, titles, and series statements has also been available.

WLN Western Library Network

In 1977, the state of Washington created the Washington Library Network, now known as the Western Library Network (WLN). This system's database is unique because the subject heading lists were input only once into a separate file, which has been linked to the file containing the bibliographic records. This arrangement has resulted in more efficient use of computer storage and has facilitated the updating of the subject file. Like OCLC, the print and nonprint bibliographic records have incorporated a number of different subject authority lists, including LC Subject Headings, LC Children's Subject Headings, the specialized subject heading lists from the National Library of Medicine and the National Agricultural Library, and the National Library of Canada Subject Headings in French and in English.

RLIN Research Libraries Information Network

By 1978, the country's large research libraries entered into a partnership called the Research Libraries Group (RLG) and formed a network known as the Research Libraries Information Network (RLIN). The purpose of this network is to foster the collection, organization, preservation, and sharing of scholarly information. In 1979, RLG developed a "nonbook system" consisting of seven databases. The film database was produced from MARC tapes obtained from the Library of Congress. Participants in RLIN have cataloged many additional items on the system. This database can be accessed by keywords or phrases.

The three major American bibliographic utilities OCLC, WLN, and RLIN, along with LC, have all been repositories of extensive data that could not be transferred directly from one system to the other. In the 1980s LC set up the Network Development and MARC Standards Office and the Network Advisory Committee to enable LC to participate actively in national network planning.

The Council on Library Resources also developed a five-year development plan for a comprehensive, computerized bibliographic system. Its Network Technical Architecture Group spelled out the requirements to connect automated bibliographic services on different computers to facilitate the transmission of messages through telecommunication links. By 1980, the message delivery system had evolved into the Linked Systems Project (LSP). In 1982, the Council on Library Resources awarded RLG a grant to create a link between its own system and those of the Western Library Network, the Library of Congress, and OCLC. The linking of these national databases has further advanced the bibliographic control of media.

The Record Transfer and Information Retrieval protocols of LSP will be used to support the exchange of bibliographic records as part of the National Coordinated Cataloging Program, in which designated research libraries work with LC to create reliable, high-quality bibliographic records which could be used nationally. Participating libraries have agreed to follow LC cataloging practices in creating records. These libraries produce authority records needed for the bibliographic records and supply LC subject headings and classification numbers. The records created are added to the LC database and distributed directly to the utilities and on tape via LC's MARC Distribution Service. LC is maintaining and updating the records as necessary. The involvement of the utilities in the cataloging of print and nonprint has meant that film and video records have appeared in the national databases much more quickly, another step towards improved bibliographic control of these media at the national level.

Other Countries

The British Library developed its own version of the MARC format to share cataloging information. The UKMARC format required some modification to the subject access system for the British National Bibliography. In 1974, the Preserved Context Index System (PRECIS) was introduced to foster the computerization of the bibliography and improve subject access to records. The Library of Congress was then able to convert the UKMARC records of the British Library into USMARC format and to insert the PRECIS strings into the USMARC 653 field (subject area uncontrolled). PRECIS strings could be manipulated by those bibliographic utilities that include this field. PRECIS strings have also been transferred with their original content description intact into the USMARC 886 field.

In Canada, the University of Toronto developed another bibliographic utility that has been increasingly popular in the United States. UTLAS has used the MARC format for its database to input 50 million records that were contributed primarily by institutions from Canada and Japan. There are 16 million unique records in this database. Many of the Canadian records include PRECIS in the subject field.

Global cataloging with computer exchange of records is becoming a reality at both the technical and sociological levels. As of March, 1990, UTLAS and OCLC are considering cooperative ventures. The exchange of MARC records among nations has aided the bibliographic control of print and nonprint materials at the international level.

THE PRIVATE SECTOR

As early as the 1920s, when film was coming into its own as a medium of mass communication, publishers became aware of the increasing importance of films for both recreation and education. Gradually, publishers' monthly film listings were cumulated at the end of the year, and subject indexes were provided. One of the most important compilations of film listings was the *Blue Book of 16mm Films*, published annually between 1920 and 1948 by *Educational Screen Magazine*. Later renamed *1,000 and One, The Blue Book of Non-Theatrical Films*, this comprehensive list classified films by subject. As films played a more important role in libraries, publications including the *ALA Bulletin, Library Journal, Special Libraries,* and the *Wilson Library Bulletin* featured film reviews on a regular basis.

From 1935 to 1940, H. W. Wilson Company, a leading publisher of library indexes, published the *Motion Picture Review Digest*, which identified and described educational films. In 1936, as part of its *Standard Catalog Series*, H. W. Wilson began publishing the *Educatioal Film Catalog*. This annual publication, updated monthly, listed films for use in classrooms, libraries, clubs, and other organizations. Films in the catalog were organized according to title, subject, and the Dewey Decimal Classification system. Renamed the *Educational Film Guide* in 1953, the catalog was not a comprehensive list. It concentrated on films available for sale or rent. Only a limited number of free films were included. Until it was discontinued in 1962, this Wilson catalog was the pre-eminent commercial guide to educational films.

In the 1940s, private industry became actively engaged in producing and distributing public service films. These free films were identified only in local catalogs until 1941, when Educators Progress Service began to publish its annual *Educators Guide to Free Films*. This popular tool describes films from specialized sources, including U.S. government agencies at home and abroad, philanthropic organizations, independent filmmakers, and industrial and commercial companies. Primarily intended for classroom use, this publication is arranged under broad curricular areas and indexed by title as well as by subject. Both the *Educational Film Guide* and the *Educators' Guide to Free Films* have used the dual subject approach by providing both curricular and topical headings. Clearly, this pattern has become an established practice. Since 1979, Educators' Progress Service has extended its media coverage by publishing the *Educators' Guide to Free Audio and Video Materials*.

In 1956, many films were being produced that were not reviewed or even identified in print. This encouraged librarian Bertha Landers to initiate *Landers Film Reviews*, which is still one of the chief sources of film information for public libraries. Subject access was available only in the cumulated indexes, and unfortunately, the cumulated indexes were discontinued. The subject heading list used for Landers' work evolved over the years and was not limited to terms from established lists like LC or Sears.

By 1960, despite the private sector's various attempts, national bibliographic control of the film medium remained inadequate. That year, a conference was held at Indiana University to discuss ways of improving the flow of media information between the audiovisual and library communities. One proposed solution was a national multimedia catalog to provide comprehensive coverage of media. This idea was incorporated into the *Educational Media Index*, which was published by the McGraw-Hill Company in 1964. This fourteen-volume publication of 30,000 media listings was arranged by subject. However, few films were assigned more than one subject, and the index was not much more than a finding list.

By the late 1960s, more numbers and types of media than ever before needed to be organized. There was no consistency in media cataloging; numerous cataloging guides were published. Evelyn Geller, editor of *School Library Journal*, assessed the situation in media organization in 1967:

> For the past few years, we have been floundering in a morass of press releases, catalogs, brochures and photographs from the audiovisual industry ... the main obstacle to the incorporation of AV materials has been the failure to impose upon them the same genius for organization that libraries... have been able to stamp on the book industry.... Librarians [should] not permit the av (sic) industry to go the primose path of the textbook field which is not characterized by an organized reviewing structure that would make textbook selection a more rational procedure than it is today.[9]

Under Geller's direction, *School Library Journal* expanded its monthly reviews of media and produced an annual audiovisual guide organized under broad subject areas. The 1986 guide, "The Audiovisual Forecast: A Buyer's Guide to New Software," listed 696 items organized under 62 subjects, which included both topical and nontopical headings.

Westinghouse Learning Corporation attempted to compile its own computerized index of media in 1970. At that time, the company was involved in contract learning with schools, and its research in the field became the core of the *Learning Directory* index. This directory included both print and nonprint materials. Each item was listed as many as nine times under every word that seemed appropriate to the indexers. Selecting the index terms from annotations and from words in the titles meant that the indexers used a natural language approach instead of the controlled vocabulary of subject heading lists. The product of their work was a Key-Word-Out-of-Context (KWOC) index. The index terms were the only means of access to the items in the directory. No cross references were added, and there was no title or author listing. The directory was discontinued before supplements could be published.

Since the early 1980s, *Magill's Survey of Cinema*, published in ten volumes in two series by Salem Press, has provided a comprehensive index to films selected by specialists in the field. Salem Press has also published additional reference works focusing on foreign language and silent films.

The database is currently accessible through Dialog (File 299) and includes full-text articles on approximately 2800 notable films produced between 1902 and the present. These expanded records include in-depth discussions of plots, characters, production notes, and more. In addition, there are brief records consisting of an abstract and a credits listing for another 30,000 films. Subject information can be retrieved from the following fields: title, abstract, note, and essay text. The subject headings can be retrieved from the descriptor field.

The bibliographic control of media continued in a very haphazard fashion. To complicate the task at hand, a new medium, videotapes, appeared. Available as a by-product of the television industry, videotapes were also a popular way to record local events. The tapes were bibliographically controlled only at local and regional levels.

The arrival of videocassette programming coincided with the realization by libraries that video, like books and films, can be used to entertain and inform. By 1976, the *North American Film and Video Directory,* published by R. R. Bowker, reported that 125 of the 600 public libraries in the United States were already circulating video materials in the VHS and Beta formats.

The early videos were available from quasi-public agencies such as the Public Television Network, from Educational television groups like Great Plains, National Instructional Television Library and the Agency for Instructional Television, and from commercial firms which produced catalogs of videos from individual producers. Local community groups, colleges, and businesses were also good sources for community-oriented videos.

A source of videos for libraries was the Public Television Library (PTL), a branch of the Public Broadcasting Service (PBS). Its video program service started in 1973 with "Watch-A-Book" programs, which included 150 half-hour videos. PTL expanded its catalog to over 2,000 individual programs which were organized under more than 270 program headings. PTL has since been replaced by PBS Video.

The name Time-Life Films became synonymous with video programming in 1973, when the group announced plans to distribute British Broadcasting Corporation (BBC) programs in videocassette format. By 1977, the company's video catalog included over 350 titles. Time-Life attempted to encourage libraries to purchase videos by offering a free color videocassette player to libraries purchasing $6,000 worth of programming. These videocassettes were available at about 70 percent of the 16mm price. The price differential has been in part responsible for the interest in the videocassette format. In fact, since 1986, almost all 16mm films have also been available in this format.

Film, Inc., a major distributor of 16mm films to the education market, also distributed motion pictures in both film and videocassette formats.

Late in 1976, the company listed 125 titles aimed at public libraries and schools. While many of the titles were supplied by NBC-TV, Film, Inc., also acquired titles from other programming sources, such as the Ontario Educational Communications Authority and several independent commercial producers. Other distributors, such as Global Village and Raindance, have distributed videotapes produced by the numerous community video projects of the late 1960s.

Initially, the availability of videocassettes was identified solely through the catalogs of individual producers. By 1975, a few reference tools devoted exclusively to video appeared. In 1975, Knowledge Industry Publications, Inc., published the *Video Bluebook*, similar to the film guide that had appeared many years earlier. This directory listed 2,500 videotape programs about business and government and another 2,500 on general interest topics.

The *Video Source Book*, first compiled in 1975 by the National Video Clearinghouse (NVC), became the video equivalent to *Books in Print*. Twenty different pieces of information from reference sources are included for each item. The eighth edition (1987) contains 50,000 pages of listings from 965 distributors. NVC claims to have the world's largest video databank.

Subject access in the *Video Source Book* is provided through a main category index and a subject cataloging index. The films are grouped under the following main categories: BUSINESS/INDUSTRY, CHILDREN/JUVENILES, FINE ARTS, GENERAL INTEREST/EDUCATION, HEALTH/SCIENCE, HOW TO/INSTRUCTION, MOVIES/ENTERTAINMENT, and SPORTS/RECREATION. The subject category index was organized under 420 specific headings. Curricular headings can be found under the entry "Intended Use" under the following terms: TEACHER EDUCATION, SPECIAL EDUCATION, RELIGION, VOCATIONAL, PROFESSIONAL, ENTERTAINMENT, EDUCATION and INSTRUCTION.

The *Videolog* is a looseleaf service that has tracked the fast-paced video market. Updated weekly, the *Videolog* has been divided into the following sections: New Releases, Directory of Titles, Directory of Stars, Directory of Directors, Adventure, Children's, Comedies, Dramas, Musical and Performing Arts, Religious, Sci-Fi/Horror, Western, Foreign Films, and Sports/Recreation.

The television industry has also been interested in controlling the medium. The CBS News Archives, begun in 1969 as an informal department of the CBS News Division, collects films, videotapes, and audiotapes from CBS television and radio broadcasts. The materials are kept both to update news stories and to preserve materials of historic value. Separate catalogs by subject, name, and location are maintained for individual film and video segments of newscasts, news programs, and out takes. Since 1975, the CBS News Archives has published the *CBS News Index* and the *CBS News Television Broadcasts* (index and transcript).

The publishing industry has long been aware of the need for bibliographic tools that would help users select media. In 1970, *Previews* was created as an offshoot of *Library Journal* and *School Library Journal*. *Previews* was the first journal devoted exclusively to films and other nonprint media. Its subject access was primarily curricular. In 1979, when *Previews* ceased publication for economic reasons, *Library Journal* resumed its former practice of reviewing media.

During the 1970s, media reviewing in general expanded enormously and gave rise to the need for an index to media reviews. Audio-Visual Associates produced the first such index with the publication of *Film Review Index*. In 1973, it was replaced by a multimedia publication, the *International Index to Muli-Media Information* (IIMMI), which includes evaluations from reviews and annotated lists as well as articles surveying media on specific subjects. In 1975, this publication was renamed *Film and Video Review Index*.

Audio-Visual Associates, publisher of IIMMI, has maintained its records in a database called Media File. This database has permitted Audio-Visual Associates to extend its services to include the creation of customized catalogs for institutions with media collections. Audio-Visual Associates developed its own subject headings because of dissatisfaction with traditional subject heading lists that were created for scholarly research and not for working librarians, teachers, or ordinary film users. The subject heading list includes both general and specific headings.

Pierian Press introduced its publication, *Multimedia Review Index*, in 1970. Renamed *Media Review Digest* in 1979, this reference work is an annual publication with semiannual supplements. A brief description of the content of each film is included with the reviews, along with the Dewey Decimal Classification number and the LC subject headings. The digest is organized first by format, then subdivided by title. An alphabetical subject index is also provided.

Review journals devoted exclusively to the video format are also available. *Video Review*, a monthly publication of CES Publishing, contains articles and reviews. A pullout section includes ten or more long reviews by critics such as Rex Reed and 250 capsule reviews on everything from classics to X-rated movies. *Videophile* is intended for the serious video enthusiast. Its video reviews are lengthy, even noting the quality of the dubbing and the amount of editing involved in converting a movie to the video version.

All new releases have generally first been identified in the catalogs of their producers or distributors. The films in these catalogs are usually organized under curricular headings. Having media grouped by subject areas is easier for both the sales representatives and potential buyers interested in a particular discipline. Broad headings are assigned, with many items listed under each curricular heading. To select an appropriate film or video, a potential user must examine the list for his or her curricular area title by title. The selection is further complicated by the significant number of ambiguous titles. The user finally makes the selection after consulting the annotation. As a result, some popular films and video are in constant demand, while newer titles remain unknown and unused.

The private sector has been represented by producers motivated by profit and seeking to find their own niches in the marketplace. However, by acting individually, these producers and distributors promoted disorganization of the very media they sought to control.

PARTNERSHIP

The nonprofit sector has traditionally resorted to cooperation primarily because of its limited resources. As a group, organizations have recognized the need to share resources and to avoid unnecessary and expensive duplication of media. The publishers of media reference guides have concentrated on developing the best guides possible to identify the media they are willing to share, especially films. Nonprofit groups sought financial support from the federal government and from other nonprofit groups like the Council on Library Resources to underwrite cooperative projects.

One of the first printed film catalogs was produced to provide access to the film collection of the New York City public school system. In 1910, George Kleine, a pioneer of the early motion picture industry, compiled the school system's *Catalogue of Educational Motion Picture Films*, in which he listed 1,065 titles. This catalog was the first instructional film catalog on record. It provided subject access by grouping the films into 30 categories.

Film's importance as a medium of communication was growing despite the financial impact of the Depression. In 1938, the Rockefeller Foundation made an attempt to develop the first centralized national film collection. It funded the film library at the Museum of Modern Art (MOMA) in New York City, which was "to assemble, catalogue, preserve and circulate as complete a record as possible in the actual films themselves of all types of motion pictures made in this country and abroad from 1893 to the present day."[10] The library was closely allied with the Library of Congress in the conversion of paper prints and in the acquisition of many early films. The film library has become the pre-eminent research resource for the serious student of film. Its catalog, *Circulating Film Programs*, has become an important bibliographic tool. Lengthy annotations are often included, but there is still no subject access.

Five years after the founding of MOMA's Film Library, the Educational Film Library Association (EFLA) was founded. EFLA's purpose was to serve as a clearinghouse for information about film production, selection, distribution, and utilization. Between the years 1953 and 1967, EFLA published *The Film Review Digest*. After 1967, the reviewing effort was continued by EFLA's official journal, *Sightlines*.

To improve the dissemination of information about new releases, EFLA established evaluation committees made up of representatives from three distinct interest groups. A film specialist, a subject specialist, and a utilization curriculum specialist were on each committee. The committee reviews were cumulated into the *Film Evaluation Guide, 1946–1964* and its two supplements. *Supplement One* featured film reviews from 1965 to August, 1967. Like the guide, it was arranged in Dewey Decimal order. *Supplement Two* covered films reviewed between September, 1967, and August, 1971. This supplement dropped the classified approach and replaced it with a topical approach. The film reviews produced between 1971 and 1979 are available from University Microfilm (UMI). Since 1980, EFLA has published its film reviews in *EFLA Evaluations*.

EFLA has also publicized films through its filmographies and its annual American Film Festival. Beginning in 1959, EFLA's festival catalogs grouped films into general categories without a topical index. By 1979, however, EFLA recognized the need to provide subject access to the films in its festival catalogs. Media specialist Mary Sive indexed the 1979 festival catalog using PRECIS, the new system she thought had the capability of capturing the uniqueness of film. Sive's work, *Educational Film Index*, is available on microfiche through the Educational Resources Information Center (ERIC). This experimental subject index was not adopted for the subsequent issues of the festival catalog. In 1987, EFLA changed its name to the American Film and Video Association (AFVA) because its activities could not longer ignore the video format.

The 1940s were characterized by increased library involvement with films. In 1942, the American Library Association (ALA) published a landmark report, *Educational Motion Pictures and Libraries*, by Gerald MacDonald. It was based on a study sponsored by the Joint Committee on Educational Films and Libraries, which was made up of members from the American Library Association, the Motion Picture Project of the American Council on Education, the American Film Center, and the Association of School Film Libraries. This report recommended that public libraries become a link between producers and distributors and community by providing information on films and their sources, assisting patrons in borrowing films, and developing film collections. The report also reinforced the validity of the traditional library approach to organizing media by subject.

ALA continued to be involved in the bibliographic control of nonprint through its various divisions. In 1978, the Cataloging and Classification Section of the Resources and Technical Services Division of ALA assigned its Subject Analysis Committee to develop the *Guidelines for the Subject Analysis of Audiovisual Materials* to provide guidance to catalogers and indexers. The guidelines recommended the assignment of both topical headings describing content and nontopical headings focusing on genre and technique. The traditional subject heading lists, including LC and Sears, were cited as sources for headings and for guidance in creating new headings as needed. Classification was recommended to "provide the unification of materials in bibliographies [and] allow for greater flexibility in physical arrangement."[11]

Apart from sensitizing catalogers and indexers to the uniqueness of the media, these guidelines provided no insight about how to proceed. More research was needed before more specific guidelines could be generated. Other divisions of ALA have focused on the physical access to media. For example, ALA's Information Science and Automation Division established a Video and Cable Communications Section in 1980 to address the problems created by the new media.

Not only were more public libraries collecting films, but they were also handling film rental from university collections in addition to their own film rentals. National, state, and local film libraries were operating in school systems, state education departments, and university extensions. These libraries shared their resources with one another. In order to do this, they often created catalogs that provided subject access to their film holdings.

By the 1950s, the spirit of sharing manifested itself in the creation of film cooperatives at the state level. For example, the Illinois Film Cooperative began by using the 9,000 films owned by the University of Illinois as a central pool. These films were distributed through the state library to all the public libraries in Illinois. The success of this cooperative led to the development of other regional cooperatives which were ultimately incorporated into the Illinois public library system. The system offered subject access through traditional subject headings in its catalogs.

One of the outstanding public library collections is the New York Public Library video collection at the Donnell Branch. It was begun with the donation of a core collection from the New York State Council of the Arts in 1975. In the early 1980s, New York became one of the first states to develop a union catalog (NYSCAT) of film and video in the public libraries of the state. NYSCAT included the media catalogs of the state's twenty-two library systems, the New York State Library Film Catalog (excluding its architecture collection), and the media holdings of the Academy of Fire

Science, the Brooklyn Botanical Garden, the Museum of Modern Art, and Cornell University. With few exceptions, the subject index used Library of Congress headings.

In 1967, the American Film Institute (AFI) was set up by the National Endowment for the Arts as a nonprofit institution to preserve and support the art of film in America. Among AFI's functions were preservation, acquisition, production, assistance to filmmakers (Center for Advanced Film Studies), film information services (National Educational Services), public screenings, and a circulating program of films. Films acquired by the American Film Institute have become part of the Library of Congress collection and have helped to make LC the largest film collector in the world.

Film centers had been actively involved in producing their own descriptive catalogs since the beginning of their existence. Since these centers were usually not connected with university libraries, they did not take the traditional library approach of making their collections accessible by standard subject headings. Local control to expedite utilization of the materials was their primary concern. Some of the centers opted to describe their collections in ways that did not meet the bibliographic standards of the library community. A national survey conducted by Project MEDIA BASE indicated that over 56 percent of the systems reporting had adopted subject access systems other than LC or Sears.[12] While these other systems might have been satisfactory at the local level, they impeded the bibliographic control of film at the national level.

In an attempt to automate its film collection, the University of Southern California developed a database that was to become the nucleus of the National Information Center for Educational Media (NICEM) catalogs. The hard copy index first produced in 1967 was significant in two ways because it had been one of the most widely disseminated film catalogs since the 1960s, and it focused on the intended use of educational films in the curriculum.

Since the mid-1970s, the NICEM database has been available as A-V ONLINE through Dialog. Having access to a computerized version of NICEM through Dialog means that subject information can be found in a NICEM bibliographic record by searching the words in the title and the abstract. Complex subject searches with Boolean operators can also be made.

Nearly 16,000 institutions have purchased all or part of NICEM's index series on nonprint materials. Since its founding, NICEM has distributed over one million copies of its various indexes. The database has been used to generate custom catalogs for individual libraries. NICEM offers two subject access options for the custom catalogs: headings assigned by NICEM or, for a fee, the substitution of two subject headings supplied by the requester.

Access Innovations and the Association for Educational Communication and Technology purchased the NICEM database in 1984. In 1986, the two produced six multimedia subject indexes: *Foreign Language Audiovisuals, Language Arts Audiovisuals, Science & Computer Literacy Audiovisuals, Vocational & Technical Audiovisuals, Coaches' Guide to Sports Audiovisuals, Wellness Media,* and *Social Studies Audiovisuals*. These teacher's sourcebooks of approximately 10,000 to 15,000 titles have promoted the use of media by grouping the items under a number of headings within each discipline. These lists have included documentaries, feature films, foreign films, and even hard-to-find educational classics.

The growth of the industry made increasing demands on the access mechanisms. In 1976, Nadine Covert, executive director of EFLA, commented on the current status of the bibliographic control of media:

> In 1943, film libraries had a problem obtaining films. In 1976, the problem is to sift worthwhile films from the glut of each year's new titles. Another problem is how to locate a particular film or films on a subject among all the materials available.[13]

The Consortium of University Film Centers (CUFC) was formed in 1970 as a cooperative venture to improve film rental standards and to resolve common film rental problems. Collectively, the members of the consortium own 200,000 films. *The Educational Film Locator,* a joint publication of the consortium and the R. R. Bowker Company, provides both bibliographic and physical access to a select group of films that has met the test of acceptance and remained in demand. First published in 1977, the locator has become an indispensable source of information on the purchase and rental of films. The fourth edition of the locator, known as the *Educational Film and Video Locator,* was released in January, 1990. This list includes 50,500 films and video available for rental from 46 colleges and universities. Over 9,000 of the titles are new to this edition; 7,000 of these titles are available in video format.

The development of the subject index in the locator involved much compromise, according to Rains:

> the consensus of CUFC members [was] that the work aim (sic) for major satisfaction to the average film user, who would like to find films about cats listed under "Cats."...the incredible feat of hand-sorting the existing headings in use in the 50 catalogs and reducing each to an entity having both a Library of Congress and a Dewey Decimal equivalent, resulting in a composite of 800 categories.[14]

Rains emphasized that a major concession was made in favor of LC subject headings. The fourth edition of the locator provides access under

615 subject headings in the combined subject, title, and audience level index. The media descriptions are arranged by Dewey Decimal Classification.

The data in the locator has been maintained in a database to expedite the printing of the hard copy index and also to produce custom catalogs for institutions. For example, the film catalog of the Greenwich, New York, public schools was generated from the locator database.

The bibliographic control of films progressed significantly with the publication of the locator; it was the first union list of educational films to give the physical location of each item. The subject heading list from the locator has been used in other media catalogs.

Meanwhile, universities were building extensive media collections which were often an outgrowth of the holdings in the film and television departments. In 1967, Vanderbilt University undertook the task of recording the daily television news for inclusion in the *Television News Archives*. The tapes of the newscasts are retrievable from the *Television News Index and Abstracts*. Purdue University established the Public Affairs Video Archives in 1987 to preserve the telecasts of the Cable Satellite Public Affairs Network (C-Span) exclusively for education and research.

SUMMARY

Progress in improving the bibliographic control of available media has required the efforts of many people. The government played an early role in providing help to libraries through its catalogs and its printed card program. Government efforts at developing controlled vocabularies and standards for bibliographic format fostered cooperation among institutions interested in media. The private sector developed specialized lists, review sources, and indexes, which they patterned after the reference tools that had been developed for books. Meanwhile, libraries and film centers worked together through professional associations and networks to identify and share their media collections.

Most of the early reference tools for film and video featured the bibliographic descriptions of items available for sale or rent. There were gaps in coverage and much overlap in certain areas because of the scope limitations of the different tools. It was not until 1970, when participants in the major bibliographic utilities cataloged their holdings online, that comprehensive coverage of the newer media became possible.

Bibliographic records for films and video have usually included annotations that have supplemented the subject headings assigned. The annotations were mostly generated from press releases, since previewing was not a required step in the cataloging of films and video. In 1970, the designers of the *Educational Film Locator* instituted the practice of previewing items before assigning subject headings. The National Film Board of Canada also adopted the practice to help in the identification of subject terms for retrieval. The practice of previewing can add significantly to the cost of cataloging. However, effective sharing of media is primarily dependent on high quality bibliographic descriptions, annotations, and subject headings best generated through previewing. Subject access methods in reference tools have ranged from the assignment of specific headings to grouping under broad subject categories. Increasingly, the reference tools have been supplying both general and specific headings, as in the *Video Source Book*. The curricular orientation of films and video has always been of interest to educators, but this type of information has been provided in a haphazard way. The *Educational Film Guide* grouped film titles under the discipline-based Dewey Decimal Classification. The NICEM indexes have been popular because audiovisual materials listed in them are organized in curricular categories. An alphabetical index is included in the NICEM indexes to guide users to the appropriate curricular category.

A multiplicity of bibliographic tools—indexes, guides, catalogs, mediagraphies, and reviewing services—has been generated over the years to provide both descriptive and subject information. In 1979, Project MEDIA BASE surveyed existing tools and summarized their findings as follows:

> As the inventory showed, those audiovisual resources . . . are represented in many catalogs and data bases of varying forms. They are recorded in varying degrees of completeness, according to the less-than-uniform mixture of conventions for bibliographic control, and are serviced by a multitude of organizations ranging from individual and local to varying cooperative endeavors at different levels.[15]

Varied approaches employed in the subject control of films and video have stemmed from dissatisfaction with existing print subject access systems. Media catalogs have often been automated without a review of the effectiveness of the subject access approach. Today, most of the same subject access systems used in the past continue to be used in media reference tools. The bibliographic control of media can only be advanced by identifying the best features of existing systems. This book will attempt this task by analyzing the subject access mechanisms of three important sources of media information.

Notes

1. George Rehrauer, *Film User's Handbook* (New York: Bowker, 1975), 21.

2. Pearce Grove and Evelyn Clement, eds., *Bibliographic Control of Nonprint Media* (Chicago, Ill.: American Library Association, 1972), xix.
3. Katherine Clugston, "The Library of Congress and Nonprint Media," in *Bibliographic Control of Nonprint Media*, 159.
4. Ibid.
5. Katherine Clugston, "The Cataloging of Audiovisual Media at the Library of Congress," in *Reader on Media Technology and Libraries*, edited by Margaret Chisholm (Washington, D.C.: Microcard Editions, 1975), 369.
6. C. Summer Spalding, "Cataloging Audiovisual Materials at the Library of Congress," in *Bibliographic Control of Nonprint Media*, 161.
7. Margaret I. Rufsvold and Carolyn Guss, "Software: Bibliographic Control and the NICEM Indexes," *School Libraries* 20 (Winter 1971): 16.
8. "An EPIC Begins," *OCLC Newsletter* (January/February 1990), 11.
9. Evelyn Geller, "Seven Ways Out of Chaos," *School Library Journal* (November 15, 1967), 4203.
10. John Barry, "Film for Libraries," *Library Journal* 30 (October 1939): 259.
11. Jean Riddle Weihs, "Problems of Subject Analysis for Audio/Visual Materials in Canadian Libraries," *Canadian Library Journal* 33 (October 1976): 6–7.
12. National Commission on Library and Information Science, *Problems in Bibliographic Access to Non-Print Materials: Project Media Base* (Washington, D.C.: Superintendent of Documents, 1979), 25.
13. Nadine Covert, "Educational Film Library Association (EFLA): Influential Force in Media," in *Educational Media Yearbook* (New York: Bowker, 1977), 123.
14. Ruth Rains, "Bibliographic Control of Media: One Step Closer," *Library Trends* 27 (Summer 1978): 89.
15. National Commission, *Bibliographic Access*, 22.

CHAPTER
2
Access to Film and Video

With contemporary film and video production burgeoning, the physical description and the content information of audiovisual materials have become useful tags for identification and comparison. Bibliographic control of the new media through descriptive and subject cataloging has been especially needed by institutions whose budgets have been cut and whose selection processes have consequently, had to be refined. The high cost of films, averaging $20 a minute, has mandated judicious buying; many institutions have "expanded" their budgets by renting or borrowing films. Video is somewhat less expensive than 16mm films. In addition, the demand for videocassettes has been so great that libraries, especially public libraries, have been spending an increasing proportion of their budget for videos.

Many film and video educational programs are produced by "one film" companies. In fact, the 1988 edition of *Audiovisual Marketplace* reported the existence of about 4,500 producers, distributors, and services for media. The 1987 NICEM index listed 90,000 currently available films and video. Today, a film may also be released as a video and as a filmstrip. About 1,000 audiovisual titles are released annually. These media are difficult to control because different versions often carry the same name. Distributors frequently acquire the films of small publishers and handle their sales, so it is important to include distributor information in bibliographic records.

The uniqueness of film and video has placed greater demands on bibliographic tools than print materials. Media are used to expand experiences, give information and knowledge, entertain, and even inspire. The visual image can be a substitute for or a supplement to the printed page for those with little or no reading skill. Media can overcome certain barriers to human experiences through the use of special techniques, including animation, microphotography, and telephotography.

Action can be shown as it normally takes place; it can be speeded up; it can be slowed down to a still picture. Media can recreate real or imagined events, actions, or processes that have occurred, that may possibly occur, or that cannot take place in real life.

Film and video are very different media. Like video, film is a means of reproducing moving images; unlike video, it is a chemical rather than an electronic process. Film is still the medium of choice for group viewing and for capturing detailed images on a screen. However, since film projectors are not usually owned by individuals, most films are viewed in public places. Since films are chiefly produced and distributed by large media companies, film programming is limited to what is available in the marketplace.

Video, an offshoot of television, is the medium for viewing both commercial and locally produced programming. An independent video movement has explored this medium as a means of artistic creation and as an alternative for providing information. The availability of VCRs in over half the American homes has contributed significantly to the video revolution. Most films have now been converted to this less expensive format and are finding their way into homes from either libraries or video stores. The growing popularity of video is a result of its intimacy and its sense of immediacy. The individual or small group watching a video program can maintain control by stopping the tape, reversing it, or playing it over many times.

Often, films are not readily available because many film collections have been centralized. The amount of information available about specific films has often been the critical factor in determining if they will be chosen by those who wish to share or rent. As a result, there has been a tendency to order only the "tried and true" films, and many items have not been considered or requested. It was this pattern of usage that motivated the National Film Board of Canada to search for a retrieval system that would foster better utilization of its collection.

Most video collections have the advantage of being housed locally. It is not uncommon today for libraries to own a 10,000-item video collection. Public libraries and video stores generally describe their holdings by displaying the video containers, which provide limited subject information—a picture and a marketing blurb intended for the prospective buyer.

Even when media collections are available locally, items on a specific subject are not easily identified. There are a significant number of closed-stack collections, even in public libraries, which have a strong tradition of open stacks. Even patrons who have access to open-stack collections have been handicapped because the collections are arranged by accession numbers, and the content is not identifiable by browsing. Films or video cannot be previewed without equipment. No built-in indexes, such as a table of contents or index, have existed to provide subject information about a title, specific film, or video, let alone a specific scene. Printed literature which may accompany the item often contains only limited subject information. Surrogate records in media indexes have been the only means of providing intellectual access to collections. The acquisition of films and video also has been solely dependent on the surrogate record access mechanism.

The uniqueness of media goes beyond the physical characteristics of materials and collections. The intellectual content of visual materials must also be given special consideration. Social studies, fine arts, guidance, and language arts constitute the content of the majority of films and video. These "soft" disciplines are so named because their terminology tends to be used less precisely than that in the "hard" sciences. New terms in the social sciences keep emerging, and terms often overlap in meaning. Also, the subjects in the social sciences tend to be interdisciplinary, bringing together concepts which cannot always be anticipated by a controlled vocabulary. The focus is on humanistic concepts that are more difficult to retrieve by subject searching.

While the greatest number of films and video focus on the social sciences, a significant number cover other disciplines. Next in order of availability are science films, followed by health and safety, business, adult education, and teacher training.

BIBLIOGRAPHIC STANDARDS

Sufficient descriptive and subject information is needed to help the user identify appropriate media and make intelligent viewing and purchase decisions. Developing standards for physical description was the first step in providing better access to media. In 1949, the Library of Congress published rules for descriptive cataloging, but these rules were not intended for specialized materials like motion pictures. As a result, numerous manuals of standards and procedures appeared to guide the cataloger of audiovisual materials. It was not until 1969 that LC published a supplement to its descriptive cataloging rules to apply to motion pictures and filmstrips. Professional associations were also making an effort to standardize the bibliographic rules concerning the physical description of audiovisual materials. In 1955, the American Library Association established a Special Committee on the Bibliographic Control of Audiovisual Materials to encourage the national standardization of media bibliographic records.

The audiovisual community also developed standards for nonprint. In 1968, the Department of Audiovisual Instruction (DAVI) of the National Education Association published *Standards for Cataloging, Coding, and*

Scheduling Educational Media. Three other editions were produced by DAVI's successor, the Association for Educational Communications and Technology (AECT).

In 1969, upon examination of the four different leading cataloging manuals that had influenced the bibliographic treatment of audiovisual materials in the United States, an ad hoc committee of the Cataloging and Classification Section of ALA's Resources and Technical Services Division again recommended a national bibliographic standard for the description of audiovisual materials. However, it was not until 1978 that the second edition of the *Anglo-American Cataloguing Rules* (AACR2) finally provided consistent rules for bibliographic description and access points other than subject for both print and nonprint materials.

The International Federation of Library Associations and Institutions (IFLA) developed an international standard bibliographic description format for cataloging records of nonbook materials (ISBD NBM). In addition, the Z39 Committee of the American National Standards Institute (ANSI), produced a standard format for bibliographic citation of nonprint materials.

In 1985, the Audiovisual Committee of RTSD also proposed that the Cataloging in Publication program (CIP) be extended to audiovisual materials. The AV-CIP was recommended at ALA's midwinter meeting that year, but the application is still limited to microcomputer software. The implementation of CIP for audiovisual materials would be a major step forward in the bibliographic control of these materials. It would help reduce the cost of cataloging and alert producers to the importance of providing standardized information for their materials to improve access and promote use.

SUBJECT ACCESS

While some agreement on the physical description of films was reached, subject access remained far from standardized in the bibliographic tools. The lack of accurate and specific subject headings renders even the best physical description totally irrelevant. In addressing the adequacy of subject access, William Budington of the John Crerar Library, wrote, "If it fails, it matters not that physical access is established, because delivery is not achieved, or is useless, or is overwhelming."[1]

The importance of subject access to all types of materials cannot be overestimated. The 1978 Committee for the Coordination of National Bibliographic Control of the Council on Library Resources concluded that subject access systems hold the greatest promise for serving information seekers. However, the committee also concluded that such systems are "the least understood, the least standardized, the least developed, and often the most costly process."[2] The committee called for continued research into subject analysis.

A review of the current literature indicates a renewed interest in examining how reference tools have been used to select materials. OCLC's Subject Access Research Project has conducted an extensive review of the traditional catalog use studies. Karen Markey, while working at OCLC, identified fifty traditional catalog use studies which had been carried out between 1931 and 1959.[3] These studies used questionnaires and observations to analyze the cataloging process. While most of the use studies focused on the behavior and needs of the information seeker, others evaluated the effectiveness of subject access systems for specialized materials and the subject control of literature in disciplines such as architecture.

Since 1980, research in subject analysis has intensified with the introduction of online public access catalogs. While the survey method predominated in the early studies, current studies use the computer to capture transaction data for the study of the subject searching process. Twenty-two such studies were undertaken between 1980 and 1984. OCLC received support from the Council on Library Resources to study the use of online catalogs. This study and others have indicated a greater reliance on subject searching by the user of online catalogs than by users of traditional catalogs.

The subject cataloging of nonprint materials has often been handled in the same way as print materials. However, the process of describing visual images is very complex and deserves special consideration. Irwin Panofsky described the process of studying subject matter or meaning in visual materials in three successive levels: description, analysis, and interpretation.[4] Analyzing these three stages shows how visual images are perceived and understood by the observer.

At first, the observer identifies the entities that are represented in the image: the objects, events, and expressional qualities, such as effects, feeling-states, sensations, and psychological nuances. Secondary subject matter can be derived from the analysis or from the interpretation of the visual image.

The assignment of subject headings and index terms for films and video has not only been dependent on the indexer's background and experience but also on his or her understanding of the visual image. Knowledge acquired from practical experience can be applied to describe images literally (primary subject matter). However, the analysis and interpretation of images require competence in making such judgments through knowledge and understanding of literary sources and film and video history and techniques. The analysis and interpretation can best be supplied by subject, cinema, and video experts.

In practice, the subject headings that have been assigned to films and video have described the secondary subject matter by interpreting the overall theme or concept of the visual images. In fact, users of collections accessible by secondary subject matter are at the mercy of the indexer's interpretation. This may explain the dissatisfaction with the application of "book-oriented" cataloging to nonprint. Karen Markey has identified the need for more in-depth coverage of the subject matter of visual materials by including *both* primary and secondary subject matter.[5] She stressed that primary subject matter description of visual materials is needed so that collections can be accessed by users who do not know the secondary subject matter of visual images.

High technology has also become a significant factor in the assignment of terms or headings. The urgency of improving subject access became apparent when nonprint records were computerized. Noncomputerized access systems allowed leisurely perusal of long lists when a user was so inclined. The time spent on a manual search for a film or video may or may not be important, and the cost of manual searching is generally considered irrelevant. With computerized searching of media, however, efficient retrieval is critical. False drops, excessively long lists of retrieval postings, or no postings at all add up to a waste of money for the patron and result in an ineffective use of computer time.

Films and video have been difficult to index. Titles generally have provided little information about the content and have included few indexable words. Fortunately, video producers are beginning to generate titles with more subject information. LC and NICEM have depended on the written materials supplied by producers and distributors to assign subject headings and produce abstracts. Since marketing copywriters have been trained to identify concepts that will sell a product, the advertising copy often has not been suitable for indexing purposes. Unfortunately, this has been the only information available to LC and NICEM, because neither organization has previewed films or video before indexing them.

A number of different approaches have been applied to film and video collections to describe the subject content of individual items.

The Dewey Decimal Classification has been used to organize many educational collections. Initially developed to facilitate the shelving of books in a logical order, the Dewey scheme was designed to relate like materials in a hierarchical structure by means of a numerical system and an alphabetical index to the class numbers. With the growth of interdisciplinary materials, the Dewey scheme has been more dependent on the subject index with its cross reference structure to show the place of any subject in the classification system.

Several of the early film catalogs like the H. W. Wilson Company's 1936 *Educational Film Catalog* were structured by means of the Dewey

Decimal Classification, the same system used in other Wilson publications for print materials. The *Film Evaluation Guide, 1946–64* of the Educational Film Library Association (now AFVA) not only arranged film titles by Dewey number but also provided a subject key to the Dewey Decimal listing, an arrangement that was later discontinued. The Dewey approach provided limited subject access because a film could only be assigned to one location in the classification scheme, while many subject headings could potentially be assigned to describe subject content. While the Dewey scheme allows browsing in nearby subject-related areas, it frequently requires consulting the index of the scheme. Currently, the AFVA reviews of films and videos are listed under approximately 150 general and specific headings.

NICEM's *Film and Video Finder*, which does not use a notational classification scheme, is arranged by discipline, similar to the hierarchical organization within the Dewey Decimal system. However, items are listed in many categories as necessary to describe the content in terms of curriculum. This approach attempts to overcome the major drawback of using only a classification scheme, which allows only one location for each item.

The usefulness of classification information was taken into account when the Subject Analysis Committee of RTSD's Cataloging and Classification Section recommended in its *Guidelines for the Subject Analysis of Audiovisual Materials* that classification should be provided "for the unification of materials in bibliographies,... [it] facilitates automated retrieval, allows for greater flexibility in physical arrangement, and encourages consistency in cataloging."[6] Since classification information provides physical location information, other indexes such as the *Educational Film Locator* have organized films by subject but have included Dewey numbers next to the headings for reference.

Summary notes or abstracts have traditionally been included in media catalogs to supplement the subject information of often ambiguous titles. Such descriptions have supplied details about the content and mode of presentation. For example, *Magill's Survey of Cinema* has provided a short abstract or, for some items, a long essay that may be several pages or computer screens in length. The abstracts and essays are comprised of analysis and interpretation by researchers and cinema specialists who have consulted and used information from several film centers. However, there are several drawbacks to relying on prose descriptions for subject information. They increase the size of manual catalogs and significantly increase the length of computer records. Marketing data is frequently presented in lieu of adequate descriptions. Accessing these descriptions is difficult in book or card catalogs. Accessing abstracts on a computer can be time-consuming and costly because the uncontrolled vocabulary of the abstract can only be accessed by free-text searching.

The assignment of subject headings has been the preferred method of providing subject access to films and videos. While the most reliable way of ascertaining the subject content is to examine the work in detail by previewing it, this method is not considered economical. However, it is not safe to analyze the content of a work by its title alone because titles tend to be misleading. Accompanying printed materials may be an introductory guide to the subject matter and cannot be a substitute for previewing. While consulting external sources such as bibliographies, catalogs, reviews, and reference sources may be costly, such action can significantly improve subject cataloging. Subject or audiovisual specialists may have to be consulted when the cataloger is unfamiliar with either the subject or the mode of presentation.

The process of determining subject headings for input into the library's catalog is a complex intellectual operation which is primarily guided by the cataloging policies of the institution. The process involves some subjective judgement which is influenced by the cataloger's background, the individual's understanding of the subject matter, the objectives of the catalog, the needs of users, and the effectiveness of communication between the author or producer and the cataloger.

After the content of the work is understood by the cataloger, the next step is to identify the main subject(s) or principal concept(s) that may involve different aspects of the work, such as viewpoint, time, and place. Traditionally, the number of headings permitted by an institution for manually produced catalogs has determined what and how much information will be available to users of a collection. Practices for print cataloging have been adopted for nonprint cataloging without much concern for the uniqueness of the media or for the lack of readily available print information about media. Textbooks on subject cataloging have focused more on limiting the number of headings than on addressing the adequacy of subject information for different media. Currently, many databases allow up to ten descriptors per item; this practice has opened the door to exhaustive indexing of materials. While more is not necessarily better, the exhaustive indexing may give users better access to media.

Different approaches have been used to build vocabularies for describing subject content. A keyword-in-context (KWIC) index can be produced by inverting the significant words in a title so that each significant word can be found in its alphabetical location in the index. While the KWIC index does not provide complete indexing, it is economical to produce and easy to use.

In the United States, the "freeing" of vocabulary (which eventually resulted in the concept of free-text searching) was started principally by Mortimer Taube, who introduced the concept of "uniterms." For searching, he proposed the use of the original author's words and the natural language extracted from titles or author-produced abstracts. The uncontrolled vocabulary terms could stand alone or be paired with other terms by the user (post-coordination) to find relevant materials. However, the process of searching for words rather than concepts often yielded "false hits," or results which were out of context. Sometimes the looseness of the natural language produced irrelevant answers or false drops when terms were linked.

Attempts to control natural language led to the use of precoordination of terms, resulting in synthetic subject headings. The *Library of Congress Subject Headings* (LCSH) is representative of the traditional standardized alphabetical lists of acceptable words or phrases that are often precoordinated to describe a subject or concept. This system makes hierarchical use of subordinate divisions and inverted modifiers. It also provides a syndetic structure to link headings and prevent the scattering of information under different synonyms and word forms. The LC system provides a structure that is alphabethical and topical rather than disciplinary. For example, the term BIRDS and TREES assigned to describe films would be separated in an alphabetical file, rather than collocated under the general discipline BIOLOGY or under the specific disciplines BOTANY or ZOOLOGY.

Another popular general subject heading system in use in the United States was built in much the same way as LCSH. The *Sears List of Subject Headings*, in its thirteenth edition in 1986, is widely used by small public libraries and by school libraries. It is much smaller in scope and more general in treatment than LCSH. Catalog cards with Sears headings were readily available from a number of sources, such as *Library Journal,* Brodart, Josten, and others. As a result, many media collections were assigned Sears headings.

Specialized subject lists have also been produced to cover specific disciplines or materials for a specialized audience. The National Information Center for Educational Media developed its own list exclusively for audiovisual materials by using the Sears list as a starting point. The subject headings were organized in an alphabetical index under twenty-nine major headings. This type of subject index necessitated the provision of an outline of major headings and the subordinate terms. The subject searcher could consult a dictionary arrangement which supplied the indexer's related subcategory choices and their overriding headings for nonuse terms. Each subcategory term was also an entry point cross-referenced to its headings.

By contrast, the National Library of Medicine developed an extensive network of linked terms in its Medical Subject Headings (MeSH) for medicine and has applied the system to both print and nonprint.

Many media collections have existed separate and apart from libraries. The subject indexes for these collections were often developed locally and did not incorporate recognized indexing standards. The lack of standardization in subject access for media in these collections has seriously hampered the sharing of these valuable resources.

Other approaches to subject analysis have been tried. In 1933, in an effort to improve subject access to library materials, S. R. Ranganathan combined the best aspects of classification and subject indexing systems then in use. While his Colon Classification scheme did not address itself to specialized materials like film, it involved a systematic process of analyzing subject content in terms of generic concepts called facets. His five fundamental facets, known as PMEST, were personality, matter, energy, space, and time.

His Colon Classification has not been widely used, but Ranganathan's theory has influenced, in one way or another, all classification and indexing systems currently in use. The Classification Research Group of the British Library was guided by Ranganathan's theory of classification in the development of the Preserved Context Index System (PRECIS). After a trial period, PRECIS became the official subject indexing system of the British Library for the *British National Bibliography*.

This subject access system has been designed to cover all of knowledge, not just a specific collection. PRECIS has been based on thesaural principles to control the vocabulary derived from natural language. This system has relied on the precoordination of terms to describe subject matter. It has also used the principle of term rotation of terms to the lead position in an index. PRECIS has been applied to films in England and in Canada.

Even though many different subject access systems had been applied to films, the library community felt the need to examine the systems' application to nonprint media. The 1978 ALA subject analysis guidelines for media recommended that standard lists like LCSH and Sears be used to provide guidance in the creation of new subject headings when appropriate. At the time, PRECIS was a new system with no track record, and it was not cited for consideration.

METHODOLOGY OF STUDY

The remainder of this book will detail results of an informal study comparing the three subject access systems most widely used for films and videos. The study will not only identify subject access problems but will also isolate superior techniques to improve access. The systems in the study include the traditional LCSH subject access system, the NICEM system, designed for its media indexes and PRECIS.

It is important to identify both the inherent *characteristics* of the systems and the *products* of the systems as applied by a cataloging or indexing agency. The systems were evaluated by examining the authority lists of LC, NICEM, and the National Film Board of Canada for syntactical structures, level of specificity, and syndetic structures. The application of each system was reviewed by comparing the subject indexing of one hundred films using the three subject access systems: LCSH, as applied by the Library of Congress; the NICEM headings, as used in the *NICEM Index to 16mm Educational Films;* and PRECIS headings assigned to the film in the *PRECIS Index of 16mm Films Distributed by the National Film Board of Canada.* The impact of the indexing policy was examined by comparing the application of LCSH to films by both the Library of Congress and the Hennepin County Public Library.

The subject headings and cross references assigned by the three systems for the films in the sample were isolated for study. A printout of film records from the NICEM database was examined to extract the descriptor codes for the assigned subject headings. These codes were translated into subject headings using a reference key supplied by NICEM. The index of subject headings listed in the front of the *NICEM Index to 16mm Educational Films* was then analyzed to isolate the cross references in use by the system.

The OCLC database was searched for records of the same films to identify the LC subject headings assigned by the library on the DLC records, which represent the official records of the Library of Congress. The ninth edition of LCSH was used to identify the cross references for the subject headings of the films in the study.

The PRECIS *Index of 16mm Films Distributed by the National Film Board of Canada* produced in 1982 was used to identify the PRECIS headings and cross references assigned to the films under study. The cross references from the index were isolated.

The task was to find what kinds of headings were used by the three systems and which practices were applied. Lawrence Leonard, in his study of consistency among indexers, emphasized the difficulty of trying to isolate the best subject headings for both print and nonprint:

> Language is imprecise with semantic, syntactic, and syndetic structuring, which may easily cause a range of interpretation of many concepts, passages, phrases and words among different individuals.[7]

It is not surprising that inconsistency occurs among indexers. Research on the consistency of indexing has revealed that there is not one right, correct, or exact assignment of index terms for any given document. In spite of the difficulty of developing consistent indexing, some attempt must be made to improve subject access to materials requiring special treatment.

A number of criteria governed the selection of the films for this study. First, the films selected had to be indexed in all three systems. Since the indexing of films by PRECIS is a relatively new phenomenon, the NFBC film catalog was selected as the primary source of films for this study. This catalog includes several thousand films produced in Canada; a subset of one hundred films was identified by choosing films distributed in the United States since these films were more likely to be listed in the other two tools used in this study. The 100 films chosen from the NFBC catalog have received 329 international awards and 10 Oscar nominations and therefore represent films worthy of analysis. The NFBC films were then searched in the databases of OCLC and NICEM to ensure that all were indexed by the other two systems.

Second, the films selected had to emphasize the unique qualities of the medium. Genre and technique are important elements in films and contribute to their uniqueness as a medium of communication. Animated, experimental, and genre films, such as children's films, from the NFBC catalog were included in the sample to examine the treatment of different types of film by the three systems.

Third, the films chosen for the study had to be films that were listed in current sources. Even though the films selected from the catalog had release dates ranging from 1949 to 1977, all are still available for sale or lease. Therefore, the sample for this study includes important educational films that are in current use.

The exhaustivity of subject indexing for the film sample in the three indexes was compared quantitatively and qualitatively. The terms in the assigned subject access points were examined for depth and breadth of indexing. Since the application of a syndetic structure to an index can significantly affect retrieval, the number of cross references used to link concepts was identified.

The quality of the subject headings was examined not only in terms of the informational message conveyed but also in terms of the language employed in transmitting that message. The assignment of general or specific headings by each of the systems received close scrutiny. The assigned headings in the three indexes were examined to identify *how* concepts were described, since concepts can be explained as a process, a resulting action, or an agent of that action. Such differences in description can be identified by examining the matching terms assigned. Different types of headings are assigned to describe content and form. This study identified the topical and nontopical (form) headings assigned for both fiction and nonfiction films. Since the educational community is interested in curricular headings for audiovisual materials, the assignment of such headings was noted.

The structure of headings can affect retrieval. Even though online catalogs are popular, many film collections are described in manual catalogs. Therefore, it was important to look at manual elements, such as the use of multiple-word headings, and inverted headings and the citation order of the elements in a compound heading.

Vocabulary

Access Points. Subject headings are written representations of content, genre, and technique described by topical and nontopical headings. The uniqueness of the medium requires many headings to describe all of these aspects. Access points not only identify the subject of the specific film but they also serve to link the different films within an index. Indexers put limits on the number of headings for economic reasons. This study used the number of access points assigned to each film by the three systems to identify the indexing policy of the respective agency.

Headings are often made up of keywords that can be independently retrieved by computer. Therefore, the component parts of the headings were examined to identify the number of significant terms within those headings. The application of exhaustive indexing is the result of decision-making at the management level. Since the terms assigned can be either specific or general, the subject content will be examined using specificity as a criteria.

The average depth of indexing was computed for the films by utilizing Maron's method of analysis:

depth of indexing = total number of terms/total number of films[8]

While no optimal depth of indexing has been established, effective retrieval is dependent on the number of unique terms assigned. The Syracuse University BOOKS Project showed the value of adding headings beyond the traditional number assigned to books;[9] it can be logically assumed that this applies to other media as well. Since additional headings can be added so economically on a computer record, a test for the completeness of indexing using the number of keywords assigned, in terms of keywords, was deemed a key factor in this study.

The average term breadth of the sample of one hundred films was also computed to identify the different terms in use by employing Maron's second formula:

average term breadth = total # terms/total # of different terms[10]

Terminology. The user of an index may perform subject searching by using a synonym of the terms assigned by the indexer. Thus, the currency of the language used to describe the subject content also deserved some attention. Nowadays, it is usually faster to make films or video on new inventions, new products, and new techniques than to publish an article or book about a new subject. Therefore, new concepts frequently occur in films first, and these must be incorporated into the vocabulary of the indexing systems. When films were added to the British Library database, the number of new terms in the thesaurus increased dramatically. An analysis of this phenomenon proved that this feature of films, dealing with new concepts rather than just new combinations of old ones, had caused the increase.

Language is constantly changing, and new ideas or concepts require description through new or updated terminology. Terms become obsolete much faster in spoken language, and subject heading lists are slow to reflect these changes. The currency of terms in the indexes was analyzed by comparing the vocabulary used in the three indexes with the vocabulary from the thesaurus of the Hennepin County Public Library of Edina, Minnesota. Hennepin County's thesaurus basically represents subject headings with newly created media headings and LC headings modified by HCL. This library's policy of regularly updating its headings makes its list a good standard by which to compare the indexes under study.

This study examined the likenesses and differences in the form of the subject headings in the indexes under consideration. Headings may describe the same content in different ways according to the principles of the subject heading system. Correlation with the user's vocabulary involving the same words or parts thereof in each index's description of a particular film was identified. Sometimes, a system may describe the process, such as in piloting, while another describes the subject in terms of the agent pilots. In this example, both terms may be retrieved from the same truncation and are described as near matches.

Syndetic Structure. The semantic relationships, including hierarchy and synonymy, are a priori relationships which are independent of the treatment of concepts in any particular item. Indexes may be syndetically structured to provide links through the use of cross references. Three types of references were explored. The equivalency references (*see* or *use*) have been used to link synonymous terms. Hierarchical references (*see also*, *broader term*, and *narrower term*) have been used to describe concepts at different levels of specificity, while associative references (*related term* or *see also*) have provided links between terms not hierarchically connected.

A single subject may acquire different names in different places at different times. The resulting synonymous terms can pose problems to the user who approaches a catalog that does not employ his or her chosen synonym. The synonymous terms used by the systems were analyzed not only to ascertain the different terms used but to trace the link between the user's term and the term adopted by each one of the systems through its cross reference networks.

Content Description

Specificity. Because of the importance of thorough description in obtaining satisfactory levels of relevance and recall, this study categorized the subject headings in the three systems by determining if they represented one of two states: (1) object, subject, or concept, and (2) class. Specificity in headings is often difficult to compare because like concepts must be compared. However, for the film "Adelaide," all three systems index geography, so it was easy to identify the level of specificity. The LC system used the heading ADELAIDE, BAHAMAS, IN ART. NICEM used CARIBBEAN, and PRECIS used BAHAMAS and VILLAGES. In addition, the PRECIS index also included the heading CANADIAN PASTEL PAINTINGS.

Vickery's breakdown of a vocabulary into facets was adapted to examine the component parts of the subject headings.[11] This method permitted the analysis of like concepts in the headings. The following aspects were studied: time, curriculum, geography, substance/object/product, action, agent of the action, form heading, and viewpoint. Evolving patterns in specificity were identified for each film to compare the headings in each of the facets and to identify the number of facets that were incorporated into the heading or headings assigned by the systems to describe a single film. Since nontheatrical films are used in educational institutions and since they are described in terms of curriculum, curricular headings were also examined to ascertain the practices employed in identifying films in this manner.

Types of Headings. Subject headings for films have provided not only content information but also names of people and institutions, geographic headings, and headings describing the form in terms of genre and technique. Genre studies can make a very solid contribution to the body of film criticism, as they focus attention not only on the similarities between certain types of films but also on the various stages of development that a particular genre has undergone. This secondary subject matter may include a categorization of films by type, often addressing form, characteristics, and imperatives of each category. The modern school of genre theory makes no attempt to establish fixed rules but sets out to describe, as carefully as possible, the purpose, form, and conventions of a type. The purpose of a genre may be moral, aesthetic, or even purely frivolous, but it must be relatively specific. If the films do seem to possess a common purpose, several other factors should be considered: similarities in narrative patterns, characteristic conventions or devices, and uniformity of visual or aural qualities. The indexer should consult a film expert for this type of analysis or obtain the categorization from reference sources. The identification of films by genre in relation to the style of presentation or the purpose of the film has resulted in a specialized vocabulary unique to film.

Film techniques also have been used to categorize films, since the "how" is important because of its ability to enhance the "what," according to Ray Sanders.[12] These cinematic headings have been developed over the years, and their use was of interest in the study of film as an art form. The analysis of nontopical headings was included in the study to explore how extensively the language of the film specialist and the librarian are imbedded in the subject headings of the three indexes.

This study also analyzed the distribution of the different types of headings assigned to determine the importance placed on topical and nontopical headings for fiction and nonfiction films. The subject heading patterns employed for film should reflect the peculiarities of the medium.

The study also examined whether LC treated films differently from monographs in assigning topical and nontopical headings. O'Neill and Aluri provided the data on monographs for this comparison.[13]

Structure of Headings

Form. The subject content of a film can be simple or complex. It can cover a single subject or various aspects of a subject. Two or more subjects can also be treated in relation to one another. Two approaches have been used to represent a complex subject using subject headings. One is to apply a complex heading reflecting all the elements and facets of a subject; the second is to supply a number of discrete headings.

This study analyzed the form of multiple word headings, since the citation order of words in the coordinated headings can significantly affect retrieval in manual tools. The efficiency of subject retrieval by computer has been established, but there are still institutions without a computer, and there are instances when a computer is not warranted.

In this study, the coordinated headings were examined by reducing them to a structural formula so that patterns in the form of the headings could be identified. Multiple-word headings are usually made up of primary keywords, or DESCRIPTORS, and terms qualifying these descriptors. These secondary terms, or SPECIFIERS, add specificity to the descriptors. Non-information words (like prepositions and conjunctions) that bind the terms together can also be isolated. The following examples will show the patterns identified in this study:

Descriptor	ACCULTURATION
Specifier Descriptor	CREATIVE ABILITY
Specifier Descriptor and Descriptor	FOOD INDUSTRY AND TRADE
Specifier—Descriptor	AIR—POLLUTION
—Specifier Descriptor	—JUVENILE FILMS

Syntactic Relationships. Syntactic relationships between concepts in the description of a subject are specific to the particular item. Compound or multiple-word headings have appeared in different formats. For example, the heading HUMAN REPRODUCTION could be listed in an index in either of two ways: HUMAN REPRODUCTION, which is the natural word order, or REPRODUCTION, HUMAN which is the inverted form. The first form would serve to relate all entries under the subject HUMANS, while the latter would relate REPRODUCTION headings. Inverted headings have long been used to build a classification feature into an alphabetical index. Since both natural and inverted forms may be used concurrently in indexes, it was important to this study to learn if the inversion was routinely and consistently applied because of the citation order of terms in manual retrieval.

Topography. Since the arrangement of entries in an index tends to facilitate retrieval, this study also examined the layout of entries on the page.

Strengths and Weaknesses

Subject access systems have been devised to carry out particular tasks in the organization of materials. This study attempted to identify superior features in the systems as well as serious flaws that require correction. The weaknesses and strengths of each system will be identified to provide guidance to librarians and others who wish to improve access to films and videos.

Films and videos are important communication vehicles. The subject access systems must be capable of identifying the unique characteristics of a film or video and linking like media within an index. The next three chapters will describe the three systems chosen for this study. The last chapter will offer alternatives for improving subject access to films and videos.

Notes

1. William Budington, "Access to Information," in *Advances in Librarianship,* v. 2 (New York, N.Y.: Academic Press, 1971), 7.
2. Committee for the Coordination of National Bibliographic Control, "The Subject Access Problem—Opportunities for Solution. A Workshop," October 18–20, 1978 (Springfield, Virginia), manuscript.
3. Karen Markey, *Subject Access to Visual Resources Collection: A Model for Construction of Thematic Catalogs* (Westport, Conn.: Greenwood Press, 1986), 6.
4. Irwin Panofsky, *Meaning in the Visual Arts* (Garden City, N.Y.: Doubleday Anchor Books, 1955), 40–41.

5. Karen Markey, *Subject Searching in Library Catalogs: Before and After the Introduction of Online Catalogs* (Columbus, Ohio: OCLC, 1984), 20.
6. Jean Riddle Weihs, "Problems of Subject Analysis for Audio/Visual Materials in Canadian Libraries," *Canadian Library Journal* 33 (October 1976): 6–7.
7. Lawrence Leonard, *Inter-Indexer Consistency Studies, 1954–1975: A Review of the Literature and Summary of the Results* (Urbana, Ill.: University of Illinois Graduate School of Library Service, 1977), 2.
8. M. E. Maron, "Depth of Indexing," *Journal of the American Society for Information Science* 30 (July 1979): 224.
9. Pauline Atherton, *Subject Access Project: Books Are for Use: Final Report of the Subject Access Project to the Council on Library Resources* (Syracuse, N.Y.: Syracuse University School of Information Studies, 1978), 63.
10. Maron, "Depth of Indexing."
11. F. W. Lancaster, *Vocabulary Control for Information Retrieval* (Washington, D.C.: Information Resources, 1972), 115.
12. Ray Sanders, "Short Film," in *Screen Experiences: An Approach to Film*, edited by Sharon Feyen (Dayton, Ohio: Pflaun, 1969), 44.
13. Edward O'Neill and Rao Aluri, "Library of Congress Subject Heading Patterns in OCLC Monographic Records," *Library Resources and Technical Services* 25 (January/March 1981): 63.

CHAPTER

3
Library of Congress Subject Headings

BACKGROUND

Historical Development

The early catalogs of the Library of Congress provided intellectual access only through author and title entries. These catalogs were mainly finding lists for books in the library's collection.

The first attempt by LC to provide a subject arrangement for the items in its collection came in 1869, when the library produced a two-volume work in the form of an alphabetico-classed catalog. The entries in this catalog were organized systematically and logically by subject relationships. The coordinating subjects at each level of the hierarchy were arranged alphabetically. This type of catalog required an additional alphabetical subject index to the hierarchical scheme. With the addition of a subject approach to the catalog, entries in the collection became more accessible to users who did not have a specific title or author in mind.

Libraries throughout the country were also developing catalogs for their collections, and catalogers encouraged LC to share its cataloging data with them. The cooperation that resulted significantly affected the catalogs and cataloging practices in American libraries.

Charles Ammi Cutter's *Rules for a Printed Dictionary Catalog*, published in 1876, guided the development of dictionary catalogs throughout the country. The dictionary catalog, according to Cutter, should provide access from multiple entry points: author, title, and subject. His apparent assumption that the user had a clearly defined subject in mind is contrary to the research on subject searching in catalogs. Cutter considered the catalog to be a finding list. According to Cutter's rules, the catalog should (1) identify pertinent materials on a known subject, and (2) enable the user to find materials on related subjects.[1]

Over the years, with the introduction of standardized vocabulary and a syndetic structure, the catalog has become both a finding list and a collocating device. Subject catalogs, however, have required the development of a subject heading list. Before there were standard lists of subject headings, catalogers generated their own headings to describe the content of items in their collections. Librarians were not always consistent in applying subject headings to describe several items on the same topic, especially when time elapsed between the assignment of headings. Also, books on the same subject did not always appear under the same subject heading from library to library. The library community recognized the importance of developing a standard subject heading list, especially for interlibrary operations.

In 1892, at the Lakewood Conference of ALA, a committee was organized to develop a standardized list. It was compiled from headings in use in some of the country's leading libraries, including the Boston Athenaeum, the Peabody Institute, the Cleveland Public Library, and Harvard University. The *ALA List of Subject Headings for Use in Dictionary Catalogs* first appeared in 1895 as an appendix to Cutter's rules. The preface to the 1901 edition of the ALA list indicated that the list was designed "to simplify the work of the cataloger and lead to more uniformity."[2] The last revision of the ALA list appeared in 1914. This list was discontinued when the Library of Congress began developing a list for its own book collection.

In 1901, LC began distributing printed catalog cards to libraries requesting the service. Since the library's dictionary catalog and its printed card program both required subject headings, LC developed its own list independently, with the ALA list as a model. LC's subject heading list, *Subject Headings Used in the Dictionary Catalogues of the Library of Congress,* was first published in 1909. Fourteen supplements followed before the second edition appeared in 1919. Three supplements to the second edition followed in 1921, 1922, and 1928. The third edition, which was published in 1928, was followed by cumulative supplements in 1931, 1933, 1935, and 1938. Six editions followed in 1943, 1948, 1957, 1966, 1975, and 1979. By 1952, LC subject headings were being assigned to describe the content of films; even so, the LC list included few headings for the new medium.

In 1966, the Library of Congress automated its subject heading list to enable the Government Printing Office to print the seventh edition using photocomposition. The availability of the automated file online meant that cumulated editions of LCSH could be produced annually. The twelfth edition of *LCSH*, issued in 1989, has been enhanced with an expanded preface, and a list of headings which have changed since the previous year's edition has been included. The *LC Subject Headings Weekly List,* issued on a monthly basis, provides the most timely source of new, changed, and cancelled subject headings and cross references. The *Library of Congress Subject Headings in Microform* is the equivalent of a new edition of LCSH each quarter. Current authority work of the Subject Cataloging Division of LC is available on MARC tapes on a weekly basis. In 1988, approximately 29,000 LC records were expected to be created of which about 8,400 were new records.

Since 1986, both the headings and cross references have also been available in the online subject authority file known as SUBJECTS. This online file includes only those headings and heading and subdivision combinations that have been formally established through the editorial process. As a result, many subdivisions which have been assigned according to the rules for creating free-floating subdivisions do not appear in the SUBJECTS file because no authority records were created for specific headings or for subdivision combinations. *Introduction to the Online Subject Authority File*, published by the Automation Planning and Liaison Office of LC, describes the contents of the file and explains how to access the subject authority records. This online file is current, while the printed LCSH is eight to nine months behind. The online file rather than the printed version should be used when recent headings are needed and when imbedded words are the key to the subject search.

CD-MARC Subjects is the complete Library of Congress subject authority file on CD-ROM. It has been available since the summer of 1988. The file can be accessed by using either of two menus to search or browse. There are two record display options: a page display from the print edition of *LCSH*, and a MARC-tagged record display. Subject heading hierarchies can be searched by selecting broader, narrower, and related terms. Specific strings of words can be searched by using the Boolean operators *and*, *or* and *and not* to expand or narrow a search. The browse feature permits access to five separate indexes consisting of all the subject terms in the database, all keywords, keywords appearing only in the main terms, LC class numbers, and authority control numbers. Quarterly and cumulated updates are included in the CD-ROM subscription.

Through the years, the Library of Congress has concerned itself with the bibliographic control of its print and nonprint collections and has made its descriptive and subject cataloging data available to libraries. Film and video bibliographic records are now widely available through the Library of Congress catalogs, from MARC records in the databases and retrieval systems of LC, in large libraries, and from the major bibliographic utilities. Printed cards are being distributed to 25,000 card subscribers in the United States and to 1200 subscribers in other countries. The Library of Congress subject access system has become the de facto national standard for nonprint, even though it was initially designed for the identification of books in a manual catalog.

Philosophy and Purpose

The Library of Congress subject heading list was developed primarily to provide headings for the library's catalog. Libraries throughout the country have adopted the list as their own. The introduction to LCSH in the fifth edition emphasized the scope and limitations of the list:

> [This list] includes only the headings adopted for use in the dictionary catalogs of the Library of Congress in the course of cataloging the books added to the Library's permanent classified collections, and is not, therefore, a list of headings equally complete in all fields of knowledge. Neither is it a skeleton or basic list which could be completed in the course of years of cataloging.[3]

A picture of how the list first started was described in the preface of one of the early editions:

> Whatever measure of logic and consistency has been achieved in the headings is due to the continuity of oral tradition, . . . and the occasional written instructions issued.[4]

David Haykin, chief of the Subject Cataloging Section in the 1940s explained why such guiding principles were not formulated from the list's inception:

> There was not, to begin with, a scheme or skeleton list of headings... Such a scheme could not have been devised at the time the Library's dictionary catalog was begun, because there was no solid body of doctrine upon which it could be based; the guiding principles which were then in print for all to read and apply were very meager and concerned themselves with the form of headings and their choice.[5]

The principles propounded by Cutter had an influence on the formulation of policy. However, Richard Angell of LC explained the digressions from the rules:

> [LC catalogers] preferred to combine elements of a dictionary catalog and a classified arrangement. The fact that the Library of Congress subject headings began as a mixed system opened the door to inconsistent decisions as the catalog grew.[6]

In the early editions of the subject heading list the introduction was the chief source of information about how headings could be assigned under this system. In 1951, David Haykin published *Subject Headings: A Practical Guide*, which focused on the indexing *practices* rather than the indexing *policies* of LC.

More than three decades elapsed before the Library of Congress issued additional guidance on subject cataloging.

In 1984, the Library of Congress published the *Subject Cataloging Manual: Subject Headings*. Its purpose was described in the catalog of the Cataloging Distribution Service:

it was not intended to be a general introduction to subject cataloging practice, nor is the theory of subject access its theme, although theoretical aspects do occur... This work is intended to contribute to a greater conformity of subject cataloging practice among American libraries and should prove especially useful to libraries engaged in cooperative projects with the Library of Congress.[7]

This manual, revised in 1985 and 1989, is the most authoritative statement on the current practices of the Subject Cataloging Division of LC. It represents a step toward standardization, even though it does not actually codify subject cataloging practice. However, as yet no section in this 617-page manual has been devoted exclusively to the application of LCSH to nonprint or other specialized materials.

New developments have continued to affect the formation, structure, and application of headings. Advances in theory and technology have resulted in changes of practice. Much of what has transpired has been documented in the introductions to the various editions of LCSH. The *Cataloging Service Bulletin,* first issued in June, 1945, has served as a medium of communication between the Library of Congress and individuals following LC cataloging policies. Back issues of this quarterly publication have been indexed.[8] Annual cumulative indexes to the *Cataloging Service Bulletin* are also available.

Over the years, various publications have been issued by LC to amplify the introductory statements in each of the eleven editions and to provide additional guidance as needed. In 1981, the Subject Cataloging Division summarized some of its practices in *LC Subject Headings: A Guide to Subdivision Practice.* Much of the material from this publication has been incorporated into the eleventh edition of *LCSH* in the form of scope note and general references.

During the last ten years, the Library of Congress has begun to recognize the uniqueness of the newer media in several separate publications. In 1982, LC released *Graphic Materials: Rules for Describing Original Items and Historical Collections.* Promoted as a standard—setting companion volume to AACR2, *Graphic Materials* contains rules for cataloging original and historical two-dimensional graphic materials (prints, drawings, photographs, and slides) both as individual pieces and as collections.

Two other important guides for graphic materials were published in the mid 1980s. *Descriptive Terms for Graphic Materials: Genre and Physical Characteristic Headings,* released in 1987, includes terms for pictorial types, such as cartoons, physical characteristics, such as engravings, intended purpose, such as advertisements, and a glossary. The *LC Thesaurus for Graphic Materials: Topical Terms for Subject Access* provides a controlled vocabulary of 6,000 terms for describing a broad range of subjects used to index original graphic materials in a variety of formats. These terms are authorized for use in MARC records. Scope notes and brief instructions for their application also are included.

The moving picture medium was specifically addressed in two additional media publications. *Archival Moving Image Materials: A Cataloging Manual* (1984), an adaptation of the AACR2 conventions, creates a set of rules and rule interpretations for cataloging archival film and video materials. The publication *Moving Image Materials: Genre Terms* provided a standardized list of genre terms for the first time.

ORGANIZATION OF LCSH

To gain an understanding of how LC subject headings are assigned, it is necessary to read the preface or the introduction to the current edition of *LCSH*. The introduction to this work briefly describes a typical entry, which is made of up of a main heading, its subdivisions, if any have been assigned, and references to and from this heading. Scope notes may appear under a heading to ensure consistency of subject usage by specifying the range of subject matter to which this heading has been applied in the catalog and by identifying the preferred meaning of the term. Since *LCSH* is intended for catalogers, the explanation provided is minimal. First-time users need to consult other references for a detailed explanation of the system.

To supplement the introductory remarks in each edition of *LSCH*, Lois Chan's *Library of Congress Subject Headings: Principles and Applications* is widely used to train catalogers how to assign subject headings. In her book, Chan devotes a section to LC practice for motion picture cataloging. Her text is extremely helpful for individuals developing media catalogs.

LCSH, as a subject authority list, identifies the preferred terms from the controlled vocabulary in boldface. A scope note may be included to clarify the meaning of the preferred terms. *LCSH* also includes cross references that have been constructed over the years under different philosophies. The symbols *x* and *xx* (reciprocates of the *See* and *See also* references) were introduced in the fifth edition, but these codes were replaced with thesaural symbols beginning with the 1986 *LCSH in Microfiche*. However, the list has basically remained the same without changes in the headings themselves. Superfluous or inaccurate references were seldom deleted from early lists, but an extensive review of the cross references was initiated with the eleventh edition. The following abbreviated entry in the eleventh edition of *LCSH* was selected to explain the features of the system:

MOVING-PICTURES (May Subd Geog)
Here are entered general works on moving-pictures themselves, including moving-pictures as an art form, copyrighting, distribution, editing, plots, production, etc. Works on technical aspects of making moving-pictures and projection on the screen are entered under Cinematography.

UF	Cinema
	Films
	Motion Pictures
	Movies
	Moving-pictures—History and criticism
	Photography—Animated pictures
	Photography—Moving-pictures
BT	Audio-visual materials
	Mass media
	Photographs
NT	Adventure films
	Africa, North in motion pictures
	Africa in moving-pictures
	Afro-Americans in motion pictures
	Alien labor in motion pictures
	Alienation (Social psychology) in moving-pictures
	Animals in moving-pictures
	Anti-Nazi movement in motion pictures
	Antiheroes in motion pictures
	Antisemitism in motion pictures
	Apes in motion pictures
	Architecture in motion pictures
	Art in moving-pictures
	Asians in motion pictures
	Atomic bomb victims in motion pictures

An additional 188 narrow terms covering the remaining letters of the alphabet are included in the list. A review of the narrow terms linked to MOVING-PICTURES revealed the use of two other terms used to describe the medium: motion pictures and films.

Thesaural symbols were changed in the eleventh edition of *LCSH* to include the following:

USE	Use the heading referred to (formerly See)
UF	Used for (formerly x)
BT	Broader term (formerly xx)
RT	Related term (formerly xx and SA)
SA	See also (used to introduce general See Also references)
NT	Narrower term (formerly SA)

LC has indicated that these new symbols need not be used in library catalogs, especially when the older codes are in use for earlier records.

In the same edition of *LCSH*, *use* references are made from synonyms, variant spellings, various forms of expression, alternate construction of headings, and older forms of headings. *Use* references are also made when a heading should not be used even if the cross-referenced heading is not synonymous. Headings with more than one word frequently have *use* references from words not chosen as the entry element. The code UF precedes the term not used in the list; UF functions as the reciprocal of the *use* code.

The codes BT and NT also function as reciprocals in much the same way that *see also* and *xx* were related in the earlier editions of *LCSH*. No matter where one enters the hierarchy, one should be able to follow either BT or NT to find the broadest or most specific term available. The following examples illustrate this hierarchical relationship:

DUMP TRUCKS	MOTOR VEHICLES
BT TRUCKS	BT VEHICLES
TRUCKS	VEHICLES
BT MOTOR VEHICLES	BT TRANSPORTATION
NT DUMP TRUCKS	NT MOTOR VEHICLES

General *see also* references are still made to refer from a generic heading to a group of headings all beginning with the same word.

Chemistry
SA Headings beginning with the word Chemical

Other references may lead to subdivisions:

Ability-Testing
SA Subdivision Ability-Testing under subjects e.g.
Sales personnel—Ability testing

The subject subdivisions are used extensively as a means of coordinating many different concepts into a single heading. Some subdivisions are printed in *LCSH*, but only a fraction of the possible heading and subdivision combinations are listed. The introduction to the subject heading list provides a detailed explanation of how subdivisions can be added to headings.

In *LCSH*, there are four main types of subdivisions: topical, form, geographic, and chronological. Topical subdivisions are used under main headings or other subdivisions to limit a concept, as in MOVING—PICTURES—AESTHETICS. Such subdivisions, which represent types or parts of main subjects, i.e., genus-species, thing-part, or class relationships, resemble entries in an alphabetico-classed catalog; these combinations are to be avoided because conflict with the principle of specificity. Some headings with topical subdivisions resemble alphabetico-classed headings in form only, as in the heading LIBRARIES—AUTOMATION. This type of heading has been used extensively by LC and is currently preferred over phrase headings or headings with qualifiers.

Form subdivisions, such as —ANIMATED FILMS or —COLLECTED WORKS, indicate the physical or bibliographic form of works. Some form subdivisions address an author's approach to a subject, as in —HISTORY or —JUVENILE FILMS.

The designation *(indirect)* after a subject heading or a subdivision is no longer used to indicate that a geographic location may follow, and it has been replaced by the expression *May subd Geog.* If the geographic unit is the name of a region, state, province, or city, the name of the country precedes the name of the smaller unit, as in MOVING PICTURES—FRANCE—PARIS. This rule does not apply for four countries: the United States, Great Britain, Canada, and the Soviet Union. For these countries, the smaller geographic units serve as gathering devices in an alphabetical file.

Few geographic subdivisions are printed in *LCSH*. The subject cataloging manual should be consulted for information on constructing subject headings with geographic subdivisions. Subjects which lend themselves to geographic treatment are treated in two ways in *LCSH:* as geographic subdivisions when the expression *May subd Geog.* or as main headings with topical subdivisions, as in the following instruction:

HISTORY
  sa subdivision HISTORY under specific subjects, under names of countries, states, cities, etc.

The headings GREAT BRITAIN and UNITED STATES in *LCSH* can be consulted to identify some of the subdivisions that may be used.

Chronological subdivisions are used to limit a heading or a heading-subdivision combination to a particular time period. *LCSH* includes the chronological subdivisions that may be used under the names of countries and other jurisdictions or regions.

A separate publication, *LC Period Subdivision under Names of Places,* provides a full list of periodic subdivisions adopted by LC through January, 1975. Subdivisions adopted after that date have been added to the list in *LCSH*. Period subdivisions can include date(s) or modifiers, as in —MEDIEVAL or —COLONIAL PERIOD, CA. 1600–1775. Period subdivisions are *always* printed in *LCSH*, as the following two examples illustrate:

PHILOSOPHY, FRENCH—18TH CENTURY
ART, CHINESE—TO 221 B.C.

Free-floating subdivisions are generally widely applied. Free-floating subdivision refers to a form or topical subdivision that may be assigned by the subject cataloger under subjects. LC included a working list of free-floating subdivisions, in the introduction to the eighth edition of *LCSH* under the title Most Commonly Used Subdivisions. The eleventh edition of *LCSH* does not include such a list; the user is directed to consult the *Subject Cataloging Manual: Subject Headings* instead. The third edition of the contains sixty new instruction sheets and a bound index. Annual updates are projected.

ANALYSIS OF THE LC INDEX

The LC subject access mechanism was studied by examining the tenth and eleventh editions of *LCSH* and reference publications and by reviewing LC applications of the subject heading list to the sample. To study LC's subject cataloging approach to film, the records of one hundred films were searched in the OCLC database to identify the subject headings and cross references assigned. These access points were isolated, and an index was created for the analysis of headings and cross references from *LCSH*.

Vocabulary

Access Points. The LC system provides subject access to films and videos through a controlled vocabulary and an elaborate network of references to interconnect terms. LC assigned 1.52 headings for each film in the sample and 2.56 cross references. The subject cataloging by LC provided fewer headings and cross references than either of the other two systems studied. In fact, LC did not assign any more headings for films in the sample than it customarily assigns to books.

Since LC cataloging is used so extensively by libraries, it was important to see whether LC practice was followed by these libraries. A review of OCLC records revealed that libraries generally assigned one or two headings for each film when using LC subject headings. The Hennepin County Public Library was the exception. In its film catalog, the library assigned 3.56 headings for each film—more than twice as many as LC assigned. Hennepin County Library assigned LC headings, modified LC headings, and Hennepin-created headings. Therefore, the difference in the number of headings assigned by LCSH-based libraries appears to reflect more the policy of the institution than the subject access system.

In his cataloging code, Sanford Berman of the Hennepin County Public Library expressed a need to assign enough headings to show fully the content, including the use of headings to identify all media genre.[9] For example, two films each received a total of seven headings from Hennepin, in its film catalog while these same films were each assigned only a single heading by the Library of Congress. Hennepin-created headings such as STORIES WITHOUT WORDS were used in the Hennepin catalog. New terms, mostly nontopical, have significantly increased the number of access points in the Hennepin catalog.

Maron's formulas were used to study the depth of indexing and to determine the average term breadth.[10] The application of the depth of indexing formula, which counted the number of words assigned in the subject headings for each film revealed that LC used very few terms in its headings and its heading-subdivision combinations. LC provided an average of 1.95 keywords for each film from the concise headings. By contrast, the headings in the PRECIS and NICEM indexes were made up of many more words to describe the content, with an average of 3.60 words and 9.62 words respectively.

The average term breadth, which measures specificity, was calculated by dividing the total number of terms by the total number of *different* terms. A ratio of 1.16 for LC headings with subdivisions resulted. This ratio can be compared to 2.13 for NICEM and 1.36 for PRECIS. While LC's subject descriptions included more unique terms, its descriptions were not comprehensive. The limited assignment of different terms under the LC system has also adversely affected how films are related in the index. With LC headings, only two films were related under ESKIMOS, and four films were assigned the heading INDIANS OF NORTH AMERICA, but each film was assigned different subdivisions. Twenty-four terms related films in the PRECIS index, while 42 terms provided links between films in the NICEM index.

Terminology. Since the currency of language can affect retrieval, the study analyzed this aspect of the headings. LC was slow to change its terminology with the times. For example, it still uses the heading MOVING-PICTURES to describe films. In fact, the LC catalogers seem to have difficulty making up their minds as to which form they will adopt for the film concept:

CLERGY IN MOVING PICTURES	RELIGION IN MOTION PICTURES
FANTASY FILMS	RELIGIOUS FILMS

LC catalogers have indicated that they have difficulty updating headings since they must give priority to cataloging new materials. The Subject Analysis Committee of ALA's Resources and Technical Services Division established a subcommittee on current terminology in LC subject headings. In 1987, the subcommittee recommended that authority records for obsolete headings be retained, if that was necessary to allow new terminology to be introduced.

The applications of headings from the three systems were compared to find out how frequently the catalogers assigned headings that were an exact match, identical words cited in the same order. This phenomenon happened only four times among the three systems. There were some "near matches," such as INTERPERSONAL RELATIONSHIPS in LC and INTERPERSONAL RELATIONS in PRECIS. There was no match at all in the subject headings assigned by the three systems for fourteen films. Two of the films in the sample received no headings from LC. Different terms were sometimes used by the systems to emphasize different aspects of a subject, such as HORSE, SPORT, and DRESSAGE. In fact, the degree of matching between LC and PRECIS seemed to reflect the traditional training of the catalogers for each system rather than differences in the systems themselves. For example, in the film *Animal Movie*, LC selected the following heading:

ANIMAL LOCOMOTION
Use for Movement of animals or Animals, movement

The catalogers using the PRECIS system assigned ANIMALS. MOVEMENT. Both terms appeared as entries in the PRECIS index. LC used a literary genre approach in its heading TALES, GHANIAN, while PRECIS organized its film by country under the heading GHANA. FOLKTALES.

Syndetic Structure. LC has developed an intricate syndetic system to interrelate control terms in its vocabulary. For the films under study, LC assigned more cross references than headings for each film. The syndetic structure, made up of *see* and *see also* references using the format from the tenth edition of *LCSH*, represented 62 percent of the entries in the LC index, which accounts for the extensive linkage between terms in the LC system. Unfortunately, users often do not avail themselves of the mechanism provided.

Use (See) references predominated in the LC index for the sample films, with almost two hundred *see* references. Yet the library community has expressed concern about the "missing links" in the hierarchy of the syndetic structure. In response to the criticisms, Pauline Atherton Cochrane, formerly professor at Syracuse University School of Information Studies, has been working on an experimental project with LC to increase the number of *see* references. Funded by the Council on Library Resources in 1982, the Subject Entry Vocabulary Project (EVP) has enabled librarians to submit to LC those access points they have discovered while using LCSH. The purpose of the project was to add *Use (See)* references to existing headings, not to establish new headings or revise the form of existing headings. This was one of the first attempts to involve practicing librarians in the decision-making process.

Twelve *see also* references, such as AERONAUTICS SA AIRPLANES, FLIGHT, GLIDING AND SOARING, linked several films together. The assignment of so few headings for each film is partly responsible for the limited number of *see also* linkages.

It is remarkable how differently the films in the sample were described in the three indexes. Even when the same aspect of the subject was emphasized in the headings, the terminology was often very different MOVING-PICTURE CARTOONS in LC, ANIMATED FILMS in PRECIS, and MOTION-PICTURES—ANIMATED SHORT in NICEM.

Content Description

Specificity in Indexing. Under Cutter's rule of specific entry, entries are made under specific headings, but "not under the heading of a class which includes the subject."[11] David Haykins, the first Chief of the Subject Cataloging Division of LC, endorsed Cutter's policy of specificity for use by LC catalogers. He stated that "the heading should be as specific as the topic it is intended to cover. As a corollary, the heading should not be broader than the topic." He even preferred the use of two specific headings to a single broad one. The application of specificity by LC catalogers was not always consistent with established practice. Since 1976, LC has used both specific and general headings for biographical materials. This practice was also followed for films and video.

This study used facet analysis to separate the elements of the LC headings into functional categories. The following facets within the headings were examined: CURRICULUM, TIME, SPACE, DESCRIPTOR, ACTION, AGENT, FORM, and VIEWPOINT. This approach was used not only to systematize the analysis but also to target keywords in the headings. LC headings tended to be concise, with a limited number of facets, in conformity with LC's principle of specific entry. For the one hundred films studied, LC's access points by facet were significantly fewer than for either of the other two systems.

LC made reference to curriculum in its headings only as a subject. Headings did not identify the potential use of films within the school curriculum. However, curriculum played an important role in the syndetic structure of the LC index. For example, specific subjects like CREATION are linked to the discipline GEOLOGY through a *see also* reference.

A time reference was assigned for only one film, *Doodle Film*, with the heading UNITED STATES—SOCIAL CONDITIONS—1969—to indicate a time span.

LC frequently included a geographic reference as a subdivision. However, for the film *Adelaide Village*, LC incorporated a geographic reference in its heading, ADELAIDE, BAHAMAS IN ART. Unfortunately, the specific heading would not be useful for the user looking for a film on the Bahamas, especially if he or she were not familiar with the village of Adelaide and could not search by keyword. The inverted form was used to denote geographic differences TALES, GHANIAN. This form de-emphasized the SPACE facet but put emphasis on the literary genre form for classification purposes.

The DESCRIPTOR facet, a key facet in LC, usually appeared in the form of single words or phrases, as in headings like CONTINENTAL DRIFT. This conciseness enhanced specificity but lessened the possibility of successful retrieval by users who characteristically think in general terms. The ACTION facet was generally the focus in LC headings, as in ANIMAL LOCOMOTION, BALLET DANCING, and CITIES AND TOWNS—GROWTH. As important as both the DESCRIPTOR and ACTION facets are, LC generally treated them as mutually exclusive. Rarely were they both assigned in a heading. In the film *How to Build an Igloo*, LC assigned the headings IGLOO and DWELLING but made no reference to construction, the basic action of the film.

LC frequently assigned two forms of the AGENT facet, people and classes of people. For the film *Boo Hoo*, LC assigned these headings, CLAYTON, CHUCK and CEMETERY MANAGERS—NEW BRUNSWICK—ST JOHN'S—BIOGRAPHY. However, for the film *Blake*, there was no mention of pilot James Blake in the only heading, AIRPLANES—PILOTING. LC always refers to specific Indian tribes in its headings, as in CAUGHNAWAGA INDIANS, the agents of the construction going on in the film *High Steel*. While this type of specificity is desired, specificity did not guarantee any link to other Iroquois tribes in the subject index for one hundred films.

Types of Headings. Film is a unique art form which appeals to a diverse audience for different reasons. Since an index needs to reflect the interests of all potential users, it was important to examine LC's use of both topical and nontopical headings for fiction and nonfiction films.

The Library of Congress has used form headings extensively in the assignment of subject headings for books, and the use of form headings for films was a natural extension of this practice. LC subject headings have a large number of literary headings interspersed with the topical headings in the alphabetical arrangement of the list, making it difficult to identify all of the genre headings used by LC. The use of genre headings was not explained except for a brief note in the foreword of the catalog *Audiovisual Materials*. Headings indicating form of the work are assigned for materials of a dramatic, abstract, or creative nature that do not have a specific subject (for example, CHILDREN'S FILMS, FEATURE FILMS, or MOVING-PICTURE CARTOONS).

LC assigned nontopical headings to 23 of the 100 films in the study sample. In fifteen of those films, the nontopical heading represented the only heading to describe the films, in accordance with LC's policy. Only eleven films in the sample were assigned both topical and nontopical headings by LC. *Monsieur Pointu* involved violin playing affected by a touch of magic. The heading COUNTRY MUSIC emphasized the subject, while the heading CHILDREN'S FILMS identified the potential audience, but no reference was made to animation. *Balablok* was assigned two nontopical headings, MOVING-PICTURE CARTOONS and CHILDREN'S FILMS and one topical one, INTERPERSONAL RELATIONS. A dual reference to the intended audiences was made in several films, such as *Ananse's Farm*, with the headings CHILDREN'S FILMS and TALES GHANIAN—JUVENILE FILMS.

LC used five standard form headings in describing the films in the sample. CHILDREN FILMS was used nine times in the index. ANIMAL FILMS was used only once, but the sample included a number of films that could fit into this category. The heading SHORT FILMS was used only three times, yet most of the films under study fell within the description of a short film. Only one film, *Adventures*, was assigned two different nontopical headings for genre, ANIMAL FILMS and CHILDREN'S FILMS. This limited use of genre headings indicates that LC does not make the use of genre headings a practice, at least for the films in the sample.

Literary genre headings were extensively applied by LC catalogers both as entry vocabulary and as subdivisions. The form headings used include TALES, GHANIAN, in *Ananse's Farm*, and FABLES, in *The Lion and the Mouse*. The remaining literary references appeared as subdivisions. The two films with the subdivision —DRAMA included the films *Medoonak the Stormmaker* and *Icarus*. *Medoonak* also received a second subdivision — LEGEND. BIOGRAPHY was used as a subdivision in *Augusta* and *Boo Hoo*. *Boo Hoo* was assigned a second literary subdivision, —ANECDOTES, FACETIAE, SATIRE, ETC.

The use of filmic or technique headings by LC is limited. Thirteen films were assigned the heading MOVING-PICTURE CARTOONS, while four were labeled EXPERIMENTAL FILMS. Twenty-three fiction films were assigned only nontopical headings and eight nonfiction films received only nontopical headings.

The study also has identified two films without headings, *Hoppity Pop* and *The House That Jack Built*, even though genre headings were applicable.

Structure of Headings

Form. LC used single-word headings to describe twenty-two films. In addition, seven films were accessed under a personal name and four under a geographic name. Thirty-three additional single-word headings were given subdivisions. Since all of these single-word headings described only one film they were ineffective in relating different films in the index.

All the headings assigned were reduced to a structural formula to identify the types of words used in headings. The formula involved the conversion of a heading into generic terms describing the functions of each term.

The DESCRIPTOR label was assigned to the action word in the heading, while the SPECIFIER label was given to qualifying adjectives or topical subdivisions. This study focused on identifying the DESCRIPTORS and the SPECIFIERS in the headings. Thirteen configurations were identified in the form of single-word headings in the LC index. Two forms predominated; DESCRIPTORS (23 uses) were used twenty-three times, and DESCRIPTOR–SPECIFIERS were used fourteen times.

Twenty-four films were assigned direct adjectival phrase headings in which the adjective was the entry word. Only three adjectival headings were in an inverted form, SONGS, CANADIAN, TALES, INDIC, and TALES, GHANIAN. The inverted entries permitted two films to be related under the literary genre heading TALES. Ethnic, national, and geographic adjectives abounded, even in a list of only one hundred films, and included headings such as ENGLISH LANGUAGE and KLONDIKE GOLD FIELDS. Twenty-nine of the adjectival headings began with a noun used as an adjective. SPECIFIER–DESCRIPTOR was the primary pattern of adjectival phrases.

The forms in use by LC today are varied and are often applied inconsistently, according to Chan:

> In the Library of Congress subject heading system, phrase headings with qualifiers, and headings with subdivisions have been used for similar functions. A time facet is expressed usually by means of a period subdivision, but sometimes by an adjectival phrase. The space facet, usually represented by a geographic subdivision can also appear in the form of a [topic] in [place] phrase.[12]

Subdivisions were used extensively for the films in the study by the catalogers using the LC system. Twenty-two topical subdivisions were assigned to increase the specificity of headings. Geography was featured in the main headings of five films. Two geographic headings were assigned for the film *City of Gold*, KLONDIKE GOLD FIELDS and DAWSON CITY–DESCRIPTION.

TIME was reflected in only one subdivision, UNITED STATES–SOCIAL CONDITIONS–1969–, for *Doodle Film*. TIME was implied in the subdivisions —GROWTH and —HISTORY. Fifteen films were assigned form headings to emphasize filmic or literary qualities. Headings with two form subdivisions were assigned to six films in the sample. Almost every heading with a subdivision had a different structural form.

In the LC index, only five prepositional phrases were used to describe the link between two subjects, such as ADELAIDE, BAHAMAS IN ART, and AERONAUTICS IN FOREST FIRE CONTROL.

LC also assigned conjunctive phrases either to join affinitives or opposites or to identify relationships between concepts for five films in the study. Some examples of conjunctive phrases are:

GLIDING AND SOARING
HALLUCINATIONS AND ILLUSIONS
FOOD INDUSTRY AND TRADE
FORCE AND ENERGY
MOTHER AND CHILD

LC used parenthetical qualifiers, such as ANIMATION (CINEMATOGRAPHY) and PLASMA (IONIZED GASES), for clarification.

Syntactic Relationships. LC indexers would often assign discrete headings to describe a complex subject. Indexers infreqently use the inverted form of headings, such as DRAWING, PSYCHOLOGY OF, as a classifying feature in its headings.

Topography. The headings, with or without subdivisions, are interfiled in an alphabetical sequence. The controlled vocabulary does not subscribe to the natural word order; therefore, retrieval in a manual catalog is limited to the lead term.

STRENGTHS AND WEAKNESSES

LC subject headings, the controlled vocabulary designed by and for LC, has provided subject access to the film and video collections at LC and in many libraries in the United States. Even though LC subject headings have been a leading subject access system for print and nonprint in the United States for eight decades, the system has frequently been a target for criticism, especially since the advent of online catalogs. Pauline Cochrane and Monica Kirkland has categorized the criticisms into twenty problem areas.[13] The criticisms expressed over the years were obvious to the author of this study during the analysis of subject headings assigned to the film sample. The review of LC practice examined not only the construction and maintenance of the subject heading list but also the development of policies that governed the assignment of headings.

Application Policies

LC has been solely responsible for the development and maintainence of *LCSH*, which the library has applied to both print and nonprint. Many institutions have unquestioningly adopted LC cataloging by adding LC cards to their catalogs. Some libraries, like the Hennepin County Library, have modified the subject cataloging as needed. However, most libraries have attempted to follow LC practice for their original cataloging; therefore, most subject cataloging has followed LC guidelines.

Until recently, LC has put very little effort into documenting these guidelines for catalogers outside of LC. The introductions to the various editions of *LCSH* have been cursory, and Haykin's guide was very dated.[14] In 1984, LC changed this by publishing the *Subject Cataloging Manual: Subject Headings*, which was intended as a guide for subject catalogers. In the manual, LC has redefined some of its policies to avoid inconsistent application. For example, clear guidelines governing the assignment of cross references have now been established. This manual has contributed significantly to the standardization of subject cataloging. However, it still lacks a set of well-defined principles for the treatment of film and video.

Exhaustivity of Indexing

Terminology. Terminoloy is the aspect of *LCSH* that has received the most severe criticisms from the library community. The primary areas of concern include lack of currency, lack of specificity, lack of rules to determine the appropriate grammatical form, and the existence of a loose syndetic structure. All of these areas were under investigation. In the past, the library has been reluctant to update the subject heading terminology, primarily because of the extensive labor involved. The terms FILMS, MOTION PICTURES, and MOVING—PICTURES are still used interchangeably, although the term FILMS is the most popular. Film is the medium for communicating new ideas, and it is essential that new terminology be introduced in a timely fashion. Fortunately, LC is becoming more receptive to suggestions from ALA's Association for Library Collections and Technical Services' subcommittee on current terminology, and more attention may be devoted to this problem.

Syndetic Structure. This mechanism in *LCSH* has been designed to relate subject headings, thereby making it possible to relate different films on the same subject. This linking mechanism has been hampered by LC's policy of limiting the number of headings assigned per films. A change in LC's policy regarding the depth and breadth of indexing for film and video can only to lead to better utilization of the resources of this nation.

LC has been accused of having "missing links" in its interconnective system. This is attributed to LC's practice of generating *see also* references on a heading—by—heading basis. A hierarchical mapping of terms, such as the tree structure used in the MeSH headings, is needed to improve the connections between terms.

In comparison to the other systems under study, LC has provided an adequate number of *see* and *see also* references for the headings assigned. The problem of linkage in this index has to do with the limited number of headings assigned through summarized indexing. LC has added thesaural codes to the eleventh edition of *LCSH* even though the subject heading list is made up of headings instead of terms. The persons involved in thesaurus construction felt that LC would have to make extensive changes in the headings themselves to apply the codes without violating the standards for thesaurus construction. However, LC deserves to be commended for its effort at this stage, because users can more readily understand the meaning of the thesaural codes, and this can only mean improved access. LC has to continue to review the list to make sure that hierarchical links exist between headings.

Specificity of Indexing. LC has been severely criticized regarding the limited assignment of headings for both print and nonprint. In the past, the task and cost of assigning extra headings in a manual catalog was responsible for LC's policy of indexing by summarization for all types of materials. Since online processing by LC has removed some of these constraints, LC should reassess its position, especially for materials requiring special consideration. More detailed description of media is needed if items are to be retrieved. Subject access to media should address the unique ways of presenting visual information. Some critics have claimed that subject cataloging by LC does not include enough keywords, let alone enough current ones to adequately describe the subject content of both print and nonprint. No systematic attempt has been made to provide comprehensive coverage of the subject matter. The problem is more critical with nonprint. Films and videos require more index terms because they lack complementary subject access devices.

Headings in LCSH reflect the subject matter of LC's print and nonprint collections. By limiting the number of headings per item, LC has excluded valuable information about the items cataloged and has seriously limited access to these visual resources, which require more description.

Users consulting subject catalogs have often employed terms that have been either too general or too specific. Yet the LC system has limited the use of both general and specific headings to describe the subject content of media. More general and specific headings should be assigned to describe media which is not "browsable" and which is often available only from centralized collections. Film and video are media that often suggest new interpretations and synthesis of known data; it is sometimes difficult to describe these nuances when the concise terminology of *LCSH* is applied.

Types of Headings. The visual message is best described by supplying both the literal and the interpretative messages. The latter is often conveyed by the assignment of nontopical headings for genre and technique. LC moved in the right direction when it published its 1988 list of terms, *Moving Image Materials: Genre Terms,* to standardize the application of genre and form terms to moving image cataloging. This list should be used nationally to catalog for film and video collections. The nontopical headings for genre and technique that have been created by the Hennepin

County Public Library for its film catalog should also be considered for adoption.

Structure of Headings

Form. In recent years, LC has made efforts to streamline the form of headings by eliminating [TYPE] IN [PLACE] headings and by cutting down on the number of conjunctive phrases used. Such changes are costly because of their impact on the catalogs of so many libraries. However, LC must continue to make its headings consistent and uniform to improve the retrieval of individual items.

Subdivisions and conjunctive headings in the LC system subarrange large files, make headings more specific, and provide additional access points in keyword searching. Citation order is not important in online searching, but the entry element in manual catalogs determines access. Elements can be post-coordinated in an online catalog to refine a search. The use of more separate headings and fixed fields would permit retrieval at both broad and narrow levels regardless of environment. The increased use of these techniques in describing film and video is encouraged.

Notes

1. Charles Ammi Cutter, *Rules for a Dictionary Catalog*, 4th ed. (Washington: Government Printing Office, 1904), 6.
2. American Library Association, *List of Subject Headings for Use in Dictionary Catalogs*, 2nd ed. (Boston, Mass.: Library Bureau, 1901), preface.
3. *Subject Headings Used in the Dictionary Catalogs of the Library of Congress*, 5th ed. (Washington, D.C.: Government Printing Office, 1948), iii.
4. *Subject Headings Used in the Dictionary Catalogs of the Library of Congress*, 4th ed. (Washington, D.C.: Government Printing Office, 1943), iii.
5. Ibid.
6. Richard Angell quoted in Carlyle Frarey, "Subject Headings," in *The State of Library Art*, vol. 1, pt. 2 (New Brunswick, N.J.: Rutgers University Graduate School of Library Service, 1960), 143–44.
7. Library of Congress Cataloging Distribution Service, *Catalogs and Technical Publications 1986* (Washington, D.C.), 21.
8. *Index to Cataloging Service Bulletins*, 1–125 (June 1945–Spring 1978) Nancy Olson, Box 863, Lake Crystal, Minnesota, 56055.

9. Sanford Berman, "Subject Cataloging Code for Public, School, and Community Libraries: A Proposal," *Unabashed Librarian* 32 (1979): 19.
10. M. E. Maron, "Depth of Indexing," *Journal of the American Society for Information Science* 30 (July 1979): 224.
11. Cutter, *Rules for a Dictionary Catalog*, 46.
12. Lois Mai Chan, *Library of Congress Subject Headings: Principles and Applications* (Littleton, Colo.: Libraries Unlimited), 1986, 152.
13. Pauline Cochrane and Monica Kirkland, *Critical Views of LCSH— The Library of Congress Subject Headings: As Bibliographic and Bibliometric Essay and an Analysis of Vocabulary Control in the Library of Congress List of Subject Headings (LCSH)*, (Syracuse, N.Y.: ERIC Clearinghouse on Information Resources, 1981), 6–7, ED 208900.
14. David Judson Haykin, *Subject Headings: A Practical Guide* (Washington, D.C.: Government Printing Office, 1957).

CHAPTER

4
National Information Center for Educational Media

BACKGROUND

Historical Development

In 1930, the University of Southern California (USC) expanded its curriculum by creating the world's first academic film department. Over the years, the USC Cinema Division prospered, and by 1950, a film library had been established to support its course offerings. In an effort to publicize the library's holdings to schools and colleges, potentially the most extensive users of educational films, a comprehensive catalog of the USC collection was prepared. Unfortunately, the handtyped catalog proved to be out of date even before it was completed. In 1959, the Cinema Division began to experiment with various data processing techniques to catalog and index its films. That year, the manual film catalog was transferred onto punch cards which in turn were used to produce the first computerized film catalog.

Glenn McMurry, an early director of NICEM, later recalled, "The resulting printout was not considered top graphic quality, but it was readable and was certainly a breakthrough in film catalog composition and production."[1]

This initial effort was so well received by the audiovisual community that the Cinema Division was encouraged to apply for government funding to continue its work. In 1964, the United States Office of Education awarded it a grant of approximately $114,000. The division's task was to determine whether a computerized database could be used to prepare custom catalogs for selected California schools and whether this was more economical than having each school prepare its own.

The Automated Cataloging Project spanned two years. During that time, three major accomplishments were credited to the project. The first of these was the establishment of guidelines for computerized cataloging, later adopted by both the state of California and the Department of Audiovisual Instruction of the National Education Association. The project's second accomplishment was to create a database consisting of 12,000 films deposited by project participants between 1960 and 1966.

The third accomplishment was to produce customized catalogs from the database for 350 schools and colleges throughout the United States. Each of these catalogs had subject headings provided by the requester. The absence of a uniform subject approach to films in the various catalogs reflected a lack of cooperation among the requesters. NICEM's McMurry acknowledged that subject headings were a problem because "most of the organizations needed their own subject headings. This was not by design or by tradition, for the question 'Would you use the service if forced to utilize general headings set up by the project?' was answered in the negative."[2] Nevertheless, the need to add uniform subject headings to each film record in the database to facilitate online retrieval was recognized.

Soon after the Automated Cataloging Project ended in 1966, the University of Southern California assumed the management of the database. In the process, the National Information Center for Educational Media (NICEM) was created. To disseminate current film information, the center cooperated with the McGraw-Hill Book Company in the publication of the *NICEM Index to 16mm Educational Films*. This 1967 publication did not contain a subject index and provided only an alphabetical list of currently available films.

Two years later, the R. R. Bowker Company published the second edition of the NICEM index, which contained twice the number of entries listed in the first edition. Subject access to the films was added by grouping them under twenty-six curricular categories. These categories were further subdivided by topical headings.

By 1976, 461,511 nonprint items had been added to the database; 108,356 of the items were films.[3] With the publication of the seventh edition of the film index in 1980, the University of Southern California terminated its long association with the project.

In 1984, NICEM was purchased by Association for Educational Communication and Technology and Access Innovations, a database company, as a joint venture. The NICEM database, renamed A-V ONLINE, remained a multimedia index to annotated bibliographic descriptions of audiovisual materials of an educational or informational nature. In addition to covering films, videotapes, videodiscs, filmstrips, slide sets, audiocassettes, and overhead transparencies, the database has been expanded to include computer software and computer-assisted instructional materials.

In 1984, the long-awaited eighth edition of the film index was produced from the database. This edition included 48,000 currently available educational films; out-of-print titles were eliminated from the print index. NICEM also produced the sixth edition of the 60,000-item videotape index.

Both editions were organized by curricular categories. According to the preface, sixty-seven new headings were added for business, economics, health and safety, physical education, and recreation. A thesaurus of 1,683 search terms provides subject access to the latest edition of the film and video indexes. Access Innovations indicated that it would also add free index terms in the identifier fields to further improve subject access, but this resolution had not been implemented as of June 1989.

The database is still being used to generate affordable reference tools for institutions needing audiovisual information for the buying or renting media. In 1986, two new media-arranged indexes were published by NICEM: *Audiocassette Finder* and *Film & Video Finder*. The latter replaces the separate indexes for film and video and describes approximately 90,000 titles in the 16mm, quarter-inch, half-inch, Beta, VHS, and optical disk formats. The merging of the tools was practical, since many motion pictures are offered in a variety of formats.

The A-V ONLINE database can be accessed directly as Dialog File 46 or in the CD-ROM optical disk format. The online file differs from the print version in that the full record is searchable, and each citation displays the purchase or rental source (distributor) and address. The search capabilities of the online and CD-ROM versions allow combining terms with Boolean operators, keyword access, proximity operators, truncation, and subject or title searches by field or record.

Philosophy and Purpose

In 1976, when NICEM was under the sponsorship of USC, Thomas Risner, director of NICEM, summarized his institution's mission:

1. To continue to build a computerized database through the encoding of information on nonprint educational media for all levels of education;
2. To continue doing experimental and developmental work required to maintain NICEM as a national center for the management and dissemination of such information;
3. To develop suitable publishing techniques to facilitate information dissemination in this aspect of the media field; and
4. To continue to experiment with, refine, and provide computerized cataloging services for media centers and libraries.[4]

The new owners have expanded the early mission of NICEM by including resources "for management purposes other than direct information transfer."[5] James Johnstone, the director of NICEM, notes that recent trends in continuing education, staff development, and training have created a demand for NICEM products in business, industry, and government. Johnstone further indicates that NICEM plans to provide more timely access to materials, especially when they are in most demand.

Fundamental to carrying out this mission is NICEM's ongoing task of identifying nonprint materials. Producers and distributors of nonbook media submit requested film data to LC on a master input form. This form provides both bibliographic information and an abstract of the film's contents. The data is shared between LC and NICEM for the production of catalog cards by LC and for entry into the NICEM database.

For media not processed by the Library of Congress, NICEM regularly checks the descriptive literature generated by 8,000 media sources, including independent filmmakers, educational and documentary distributors, and television broadcasters. NICEM regularly reviews the media catalogs of major educational institutions, and garners additional information on films produced and distributed on a regional basis through involvement in custom catalogs it produces for film centers and libraries throughout the United States.

To foster the dissemination of audiovisual information in its print indexes, NICEM developed a dual system of data management, providing access by title and subject. Full bibliographic information for films is provided under the title. Steve Sicard, indexing consultant to NICEM, indicated that the *Sears List of Subject Headings* was initially used to assign subject headings to the films in the database. Subsequently, the subject headings were modified into a curricular scheme described in the Subject Heading Outline. The Index to Subject Headings was designed to provide entry into the scheme. Sicard stressed that the NICEM headings are "unique" in their orientation and have been designed "for teachers, not librarians."[6]

Sicard also indicated that the updating of the NICEM subject headings was based on NICEM's research and user request. The NICEM research approach at USC was described in detail in the spring, 1979, *NICEM Newsletter*. The newsletter stated that the 1979 index changes were recommended by the NICEM staff and then examined through "an informal online full text computer search of the NICEM database . . . to ascertain the approximate number of entries which could use a given heading."[7] The results were examined by Steve Sicard, who recommended a number of additional changes based on his observation of the deficiencies of the subject index. After careful consideration, accepted changes were incorporated into the NICEM subject index.

ORGANIZATION OF THE NICEM INDEX

Volume 1 includes a brief introduction to the subject access system and is followed by the Subject Heading Outline, the Index to Subject Headings, and the Subject Guide. The three remaining volumes of the printed index to films are organized alphabetically by title. Complete bibliographic information on each item can be obtained from this listing. However, the records do not include reference to the curriculum categories to which each item is assigned.

In the introductory pages of Volume 1 of the NICEM *Film & Video Finder*, there is an explanation of how the list is organized and how films and video can be retrieved by title or subject. While NICEM's rules for the development of its subject headings are not explained, the volume does provide a subject heading list, Subject Heading Outline. This outline gives an overview of the twenty-six curriculum areas or categories and the topical subheadings under the various categories in use in the NICEM index. Under the category ENGLISH LANGUAGE, for example, nineteen subheadings or sub-categories are listed that are used in the index to organize the films and videos in this discipline:

ENGLISH LANGUAGE
    ENGLISH LANGUAGE—GENERAL
    ENGLISH LANGUAGE—STUDY AND TEACHING
    ENGLISH LANGUAGE FOR FOREIGNERS
    GRAMMAR
    LINGUISTICS
    READING AND EXPRESSION
    READING COMPREHENSION
    READING INSTRUCTION
    SPEECH—GENERAL
    SPEECH—DISCUSSION TECHNIQUES
    SPEECH—LISTENING
    SPEECH—PHONICS
    SPEECH—PRONUNCIATION
    SPEECH—STUDY AND TEACHING
    SPEECH—VOICE
    VOCABULARY—GENERAL
    VOCABULARY—ALPHABET
    VOCABULARY—SPELLING
    WRITING

With specific headings related to each curricular area, a quasi-classified scheme results. The Index of Subject Headings complements the scheme by providing an alphabetical list of terms in the categories of the scheme. For example, this index lists the topic COLOR. Under this topic, films are listed in two categories: FINE ARTS or SCIENCE—PHYSICAL. Within the category FINE ARTS, films on color can be found under the subheading ART. Within the category SCIENCE—PHYSICAL, films on color can be found under two subheadings, BASIC PHYSICAL SCIENCE—LIGHT AND COLOR and

PHYSICS—LIGHT AND COLOR. Science films on a subject are often listed under two science subheadings.

Unstated in the directions on how to use the index is the old NICEM policy of segregating films by grade level. BASIC PHYSICAL SCIENCE was a category restricted to elementary-level films, while PHYSICS was intended for students at the secondary level.[8]

The primary purpose of the Index to Subject Headings is to provide a link between terms and items listed. There is no apparent hierarchy of concepts in the terms in this index. In some instances, specific terms are included to describe concepts; at other times, only general terms appear in the index to describe topics or concepts. This lack of pattern or consistency in subject breakdown is evident in the subheadings listed under the category AGRICULTURE: CROPS, ENGINEERING, FOREIGN, HISTORY, LIVESTOCK, RESEARCH, SOCIETIES, and STATISTICS.

When the curricular category and the specific subdivisions under that category are known, it is easy to locate films that fit a particular description. The subject guide includes a listing of titles under each term. The audience level and the distribution code are also provided next to each title for preselection.

ANALYSIS OF INDEX

The headings and the cross references in the index were examined to determine the scope, vocabulary, strengths, and limitations of the NICEM system.

Vocabulary

Access Points. The greater the number of subject headings assigned, the greater the probability that a user's term will match an entry term in the index. Therefore it was important to identify the number of access points in the NICEM index. Carol Mandel, in her study conducted for the Council on Library Resources, reported that users often select terms that are either too broad or too narrow.[9] Therefore the assignment of both general and specific access points would be desirable, especially since media is not readily accessible or "browsable."

Based on this information, the number of subject headings assigned for each film was tallied, and the specificity of the headings was determined to identify the adequacy of subject coverage for the films in the NICEM index.

In the hard copy index, the following was a single entry and a single access point:

SCIENCE—NATURAL
BASIC LIFE SCIENCE, ANIMALS—PETS

However, when the keywords were taken into account, this same entry provided four access points that could be retrieved in an online system: SCIENCE—NATURAL, BASIC LIFE SCIENCE, ANIMALS, and PETS.

For the 100 films studied, NICEM assigned 3.78 subject headings for each film. NICEM compared very favorably to LC's average of 1.52 headings and PRECIS' 2.78 headings. NICEM assigned as many as five to eight headings each to 31 of the 100 films under study. The NICEM headings were assigned to films for entry into the database, which permitted the addition of headings at very little extra cost.

When the keywords in the headings were tallied, the access points for the three systems were increased as follows: NICEM, 9.62 words for each film; PRECIS, 3.60 words; and LC, 1.95 words. The depth of indexing in the NICEM index seemed impressive until the breadth was calculated. Although 962 keywords were used by NICEM to describe the 100 sample films, only 450 of the keywords were unique.

The NICEM indexers tended to use general words to describe the films. This is in sharp contrast to the practice of LC and PRECIS of assigning unique and highly specific terms. NICEM's treatment of the film *Blades and Brass* was representative, with two general headings and one specific heading:

PHYSICAL EDUCATION AND RECREATION
ATHLETICS
SPORTS—GENERAL
HOCKEY

An overview of NICEM's subject headings assigned to the films in the sample confirmed this observation. For example, there were 54 instances in which films were classified under the subject heading SOCIOLOGY. There were 21 references to SOCIAL PSYCHOLOGY and eleven references to SOCIAL GUIDANCE AND COUNSELING.

Not only were the general curricular headings assigned liberally, but NICEM assigned topical keywords liberally as well. For example, 16 of the 100 films studied were linked to the term HUMAN RELATIONS. Fourteen references were made to the heading INDIANS OF NORTH AMERICA and its seven subheadings.

NICEM's practice of assigning similar headings may in part explain why there are so many titles under each heading in the database. A search of the NICEM database on November 5, 1981, revealed an unusually large number of postings for each search term. The printed index was first consulted to identify the appropriate search terms for one of the films in the sample, *About Puberty and Reproduction*. There was an entry under the term ADOLESCENT DEVELOPMENT which made reference to subdivisions under EDUCATION and PSYCHOLOGY. No entry or cross reference appeared under the word "puberty" in the index. Under the term REPRODUCTION (HUMAN), two categories were listed with films on the subject:

SCIENCE (NATURAL)
    BASIC LIFE SCIENCE, HUMAN BEINGS
    GROWTH AND DEVELOPMENT

    BIOLOGY, PHYSIOLOGY (HUMAN)
    REPRODUCTION

The following terms were then queried online:

Term or Code	Postings
MC = MP (MOTION PICTURES)	87,632
PUBERTY/DE (DESCRIPTOR)	0
REPRODUCTION/DE	1,179
GROWTH AND DEVELOPMENT/DE	3,074
PHYSIOLOGY/DE	6,624
NATURAL (W) SCIENCE/DE	0
SCIENCE/DE	43,076
ADOLESCENCE/DE	975
NATIONAL FILM BOARD OF CANADA	2,735

Because there were so many postings under each term, the combining of individual concepts through the use of Boolean operators was required to limit the output.

Terminology. NICEM used Sears as the basis for the initial generation of subject headings. Current headings are added as needed and limited references are provided to synonyms.

There was no apparent attempt to focus on the language of the films themselves; instead the films are described exclusively in terms of the curriculum taught in the schools.

Syndetic Structure. A number of headings were introduced into the subject index to compensate for multiple word subheadings, such as ENERGY AND MATTER, or RIVERS, LAKES, AND OCEANS. In many cases, no cross references linked popular and scientific terms, different language terms, or opposites. The greatest use of cross references in NICEM involved links to broader terms. For example, the term AIRPLANES provided a lead to AVIATION, while CHRISTMAS was linked to the headings in use in the system: HOLIDAYS—RELIGIOUS and CHRISTIANITY. A film on frogs could be found in the index under FROG, AMPHIBIANS, or ANIMALS. However, a film on cats could only be located under entries for PETS and ANIMALS; there was no entry under CATS. The cross references appeared to have been generated on a film by film basis, without the application of established guidelines for linking the terms hierarchically.

Content Description

Specificity of Indexing. The specificity of NICEM headings was studied by examining their elemental structure and breaking the words in the headings into the following facets: CURRICULUM, TIME, SPACE, SUBSTANCE/OBJECT/PRODUCT, ACTION, AGENT, FORM and VIEWPOINT. Similar facets in the different systems could then be compared.

Since NICEM provided more access points by facets than the other systems it was important to analyze the type of information within the facets themselves. NICEM assigned a minimum of one curricular heading for each film. However, the film *Zikkaron* had seven curricular headings, with four main categories, FINE ARTS, LITERATURE AND DRAMA, RELIGION AND PHILOSOPHY, and SCIENCE–NATURAL, and three curricular subdivisions, PHILOSOPHY, BIOLOGY, and ZOOLOGY.

Some films in the index did not fall neatly into any of the twenty-six categories used by NICEM for curricular division; subject retrieval of these films was seriously affected. For example, the film *Hunger* was listed under BUSINESS AND ECONOMICS, ECONOMIC GEOGRAPHY, GUIDANCE AND COUNSELING, HEALTH & SAFETY, and SOCIOLOGY. Moreover, seven headings were assigned to the film by NICEM, but none made reference to the film's mode of exposition, namely, an animated film without words. However, this extensive list of curricular headings assigned to *Hunger* specified potential use rather than content description.

By contrast to the practices of the other systems under study, NICEM excluded all dates in the headings, thereby foregoing the TIME facet altogether.

NICEM's geographic headings are usually general in nature. For example, CARIBBEAN was selected as a heading for the film *Adelaide* instead of the specific term, BAHAMAS. Generally, references to geography occur on a hit-or-miss basis. In the NICEM index, the headings HISTORY and GEOGRAPHY were subdivided only into WORLD and UNITED STATES. This same type of provincialism was exhibited in the headings AMERICAN BIOGRAPHY and FOREIGN BIOGRAPHY. Unfortunately, the –WORLD and –FOREIGN subheadings linked far too many films; at the least, a breakdown by continent is needed to improve retrieval of films dealing with non-U.S. subjects.

The SUBSTANCE/OBJECT/PRODUCT facets in the NICEM subject headings were often very broad: HOLIDAYS for a film on Christmas; HOME AND SCHOOL for a film on an igloo. NICEM needs to consider increasing the specificity of its headings through the use of more exact words and phrases. NICEM might also investigate the possibility of decreasing its nonspecific headings. For example, HUMAN RELATIONS and DISCRIMINATION were very descriptive for the film *Balabok*, but the additional heading ATTITUDES AND ADJUSTMENT did not add sufficient meaning.

The examination of NICEM headings for the ACTION facet revealed that NICEM had chosen general terms as action words: CULTURE AND SOCIAL PROCESSES and GROUP AND INTERPERSONAL PROCESSES. Some specific action words like CREATIVITY, ADAPTATION, CONSTRUCTION, and DISCOVERY AND EXPLORATION also appeared as headings. Action terms have been useful in subject retrieval; more of them are needed in the NICEM index.

The AGENT facet played an insignificant role in the headings assigned by NICEM. The only reference to people was made in the headings AMERICAN BIOGRAPHY (OTHER THAN PRESIDENT and FOREIGN BIOGRAPHY. Personal names were never added as entries. NICEM also made no references to the VIEWPOINT facet in its headings.

There was no match for the subject headings assigned by the three systems for fourteen films. In part the lack of matches is attributable to the absence of systematic approaches for analyzing subject content. If facet analysis had been adopted, there would have been more matches among the subject headings assigned.

Types of Headings. The NICEM headings included a curriculum category followed by either a topical subheading describing content or a nontopical subheading with an emphasis on filmic or literary qualities. Forty films in the sample were assigned nontopical headings, reflecting the uniqueness of the medium. NICEM's nontopical headings are clearly divided into literary genre and media techniques. The headings CHILDREN'S STORIES and FOLKLORE were used for eight different films in the study. The following literary headings were used to a lesser extent:

ALLEGORY	MYTHOLOGY
FABLES	SAGAS
FAIRY TALES	SATIRE
FICTION	SHORT FICTION
LITERATURE, CLASSICAL	SHORT STORY
LITERATURE—OTHER COUNTRIES	

In its Subject Heading Outline, NICEM devoted two curricular categories to nontopical characteristics, FINE ARTS and INDUSTRIAL & TECHNICAL EDUCATION. The MOTION PICTURE division of FINE ARTS was further subdivided into the following terms: GENERAL, ANIMATED SHORT, EXPERIMENTAL, FILM AS ART and SHORT FICTION. Nineteen of the films were linked to either GENERAL or ANIMATED SHORTS. Three of the films were singled out for the FILM AS ART listing, and only one for SHORT FICTION. Only two films, *Neighbors* and *Pas de Deux*, were termed EXPERIMENTAL.

The INDUSTRIAL AND TECHNICAL EDUCATION category had a major section devoted to PHOTOGRAPHY. Only three films were listed under it. This section was in turn subdivided into five areas, GENERAL, ANIMATION, COMPUTER-GENERATED, EXPERIMENTAL, and MOTION PICTURE PHOTOGRAPHY. The distinction between the art and technical education categories was unclear, especially since some films were assigned headings from both categories. The film *Hunger* received three headings with an emphasis on animation: MOTION PICTURE—ANIMATED SHORT; PHOTOGRAPHY, ANIMATION, and PHOTOGRAPHY, COMPUTER ANIMATED.

Structure of Headings

Form. The headings assigned in the NICEM index were studied to determine their grammatical structure because of the effect on the citation order of words in the headings. Most of the categories in NICEM are expressed as single words, but topical headings are frequently expressed as phrases. NICEM used twenty-seven adjectival phrase headings. The lead adjective, often comprised of such nondescript terms as personal, social, natural, or public, conveyed little information about the film.

Headings with subdivisions are commonly used in the NICEM index. The subdivision—GENERAL is used to subdivide both curricular and topical aspects of the headings. Thirty-one such headings were so assigned, as in MUSIC—GENERAL and HUMAN BODY—GENERAL. The forms used for headings with subdivisions were so varied as to indicate that such headings were created without any regard to form. Only two prepositional phrases were used in the NICEM index: as a heading in SYMBOLISM IN LITERATURE, and as a subdivision in —FILM AS ART. Conjunctive phrases were used to join affinitives by the NICEM system twenty times. Related concepts were frequently "anded," as in FRONTIER AND EXPLORATION, WIT AND HUMOR and VOYAGES AND TRAVEL. Phrases also express relationships, as in ARTISTS AND THEIR WORK, FOOD AND COOKING, DATING AND COURTSHIP and FOOD ADULTERATION AND INSPECTION.

Syntactical Relationships. Inverted headings were in use twenty-seven times in the index for the sample. There were few references in the index to the adopted form or to the natural language form. The punctuation used to identify the inversion varied so that no apparent pattern was identified. PSYCHOLOGY was subdivided by qualifying adjectives preceded by a comma: PSYCHOLOGY, ANIMAL, PSYCHOLOGY, CLINICAL, and PSYCHOLOGY, SOCIAL. Other headings, like SCIENCE, were separated by a dash: SCIENCE—NATURAL and SCIENCE—PHYSICAL. Two inverted phrases used parenthetical qualifiers: INTEGRATION (ETHNIC) and PSYCHOLOGY (HUMAN). In a few cases, two approaches were used for the same heading: MUSIC—INSTRUMENTAL and MUSIC, INSTRUMENTAL.

While many subheadings were assigned to a film, there was no attempt to link them to other topics on the subject.

Topography. The layout of headings was very structured, with the films listed under the various subheadings grouped into twenty-six categories.

STRENGTHS AND WEAKNESSES

The analysis of the NICEM system was undertaken prior to 1985, before changes were made by the new owners, Access Innovations and AECT. However, the results are still valid because the basic organization of the system has remained unchanged.

Application Policies

The NICEM system was developed to provide intellectual access to a database of educational media. The indexers sought to link media to curriculum, a need frequently expressed by the educational community. With that basic premise, the indexers created a topical breakdown under each of the twenty-six categories. The plan had merit, but unfortunately it was not developed with sufficient detail for consistent application by the system.

The indexing guidelines were never published. Indexing patterns were not always identifiable or consistent. The subject index also did not include personal names or names of programs as a subject. This information may be included in an identifier field, but it may not be retrievable by subject searching. For example, the process of identifying the four films in the database on the Montessori method of teaching was complex simply because the popular subject was not identified by name. In addition, the only guidance available to the user of the media indexes is provided through a cursory introduction in the front section of the print indexes.

The bibliographic record for a known film would logically list subject headings so users could identify other films on the subject. Unfortunately, bibliographic records in the manual index do not include the headings assigned. Fortunately, the computer record includes both the assigned headings and the appropriate numeric code.

Exhaustivity in Indexing

Access Points. The designers of the NICEM index recognized the importance of assigning many headings to describe films and videos. The NICEM practice of assigning many headings has helped to popularize the index. Unfortunately, the index focused primarily on curricular aspects. After pigeonholing media in categories, the indexers then assigned only the topical or nontopical subdivisions under the selected categories. If the access points provided had been specific enough to cover the different aspects of the subject, the subject retrieval would have made the NICEM index truly superior. This bibliographic tool can be criticized for its overemphasis on curricular organization at the expense of adequate subject content. By limiting the subject information for films and video, NICEM has failed to recognize that the end-user may be able to identify other creative uses from adequate subject information.

Since many keywords were assigned to each film, many films in the index were linked to each other. However, linkages are useful only when they identify specific relationships. Unfortunately, the frequent use of general terms in the NICEM index linked so many films together that users would be required to further narrow their search results by reading the annotations or combining terms to refine the search.

Since film and video are media that often introduce new ideas and new labels for these ideas, one would expect to find many current terms in use in a system devoted exclusively to media. Instead, the terms in the NICEM list describe traditional disciplines and topics within the curriculum. Since films and videos are not previewed by NICEM indexers before they are entered into the database, the current terms in the films were not identified for consideration as retrieval terms.

Specificity of Indexing. The lack of specificity in the headings has been one of the major drawbacks of this system. Too many films in the sample under study were grouped under a limited number of general terms within curricular categories. Tests have shown that readers react negatively to more than twenty entries under a heading and will not follow them all the way through. There are five hundred films on atomic and nuclear energy in the index, but the system offers no way to distinguish among them. In addition, the scheme of categories was especially inadequate for handling multidisciplinary films. While a list of films and videos can be easily browsed in a book index, such as the print version of *Film & Video Finder*, the printing of that long list during computer searching can be both frustrating and expensive. Consequently, the database user has to rely on complex search strategies to limit the output. The use of the NICEM database on CD-ROM is recommended to permit the manipulation required to obtain the desired output without incurring additional costs attributable to the inadequacies of the system. There is a need to systematically eliminate the very broad headings to improve the precision of the subject searching in this system. The listing under general headings has led to high recall but low precision. The lack of specific headings to describe a film in the index may account for the fact that the terms used in the NICEM index rarely agreed with the terms in the other two indexes.

Types of Headings. The topical headings under each category are very limited in number; therefore, searching under curricular categories is required. Films on the aging process and the aging population were all grouped together under GERIATRICS (OLD AGE), thus making it necessary for the user to view these films to be able to identify the aspect of the topic covered. In addition, the breakdown under each discipline is usually not uniform and consistent. The following topical subdivisions under the category SOCIOLOGY are either very general or very specific: MANNERS AND CUSTOMS, PRISONS, PUNISHMENT, and WOMEN—RIGHTS OF WOMEN. There is no discernible pattern to how and why they were created.

The NICEM system includes nontopical headings to describe genre and technique in two categories: INDUSTRIAL AND TECHNICAL EDUCATION and PHOTOGRAPHY. Genre headings are given a literary slant, while the technique headings seemed to focus more on technology than on visual effect. The nontopical headings are not standardized, and there are no recognizable pattern of application. Nontopical aspects deserve more comprehensive treatment.

Structure of Headings

The early use of the *Sears Subject Heading List* was no longer in evidence when the subject headings were examined. The extensive use of conjunctive phrases has decreased the specificity of the headings and has seriously limited the usefulness of NICEM. There are too many of these headings, which has contributed to their general nature, as in SPACE AND SOLAR SYSTEM, and CONSERVATION AND NATURAL RESOURCES. The precoordination of headings in this fashion yielded general headings and as a result, far too many films were assigned the same heading.

Overcoming the serious handicaps in this system would require a major overhaul to improve the intellectual access to specific films or videos in the database. This index is valuable for curricular information, but its treatment of subject content is totally inadequate.

There is a need to address the subject content before identifying the curricular orientation of media. Users of the database have found it difficult to locate other films on the same subject due to the almost nonexistent syndetic structure. Research on the use of catalogs has indicated the importance of *see* and *see also* references to help the user identify the term selected by the system to describe a concept.

It is unfortunate that the bibliographic records in the printed version of the index do not include the assigned headings. This subject information is worth the added printing cost because the information can help the user identify other media on the same subject.

Notes

1. Glenn McMurry, "National Information Center for Educational Media," in *Bibliographic Control of Nonprint Media*, edited by Pearce Grove and Evelyn Clement (Chicago: American Library Association, 1972), 184.
2. Ibid., 185.
3. Thomas Risner, "NICEM: National Information Center for Educational Media—A Brief Overview," in *Educational Media Yearbook, 1977*, edited by James Brown (Ann Arbor, Mich.: Bowker, 1978), 26.
4. Ibid., 25.
5. James Johnstone, "Second Look: A-V ONLINE—An Early File Revitalized," *Database* 8, no. 2 (June 1985): 55.
6. Steve Sicard, consultant to NICEM, telephone interview with investigator, April 5, 1982.
7. *NICEM Newsletter* 1 (Spring 1979): 1.
8. Sicard, interview.
9. Carol Mandel, *Subject Access in the Online Catalogs, A Report for the Council on Library Resources* (Washington, D.C.: Council on Library Resources, 1981), 23.

CHAPTER

5
Preserved Context Index System

BACKGROUND

Historical Development

During the last three decades, efforts have been made on an international level to standardize and computerize cataloging records. Many countries, including England, have adopted some version of the MARC format to facilitate the sharing of bibliographic records. When the UKMARC format was used to produce the *British National Bibliography*, the PREserved Context Index System (PRECIS) was selected to provide subject access to the print and nonprint entries in the bibliography.

Since 1951, a variant version of the Dewey Decimal Classification (DDC) has been used to produce a chain index to this classified bibliography in which the citation order is hierarchically based on the Dewey Decimal system. Items listed in the bibliography were assigned as many classification numbers as necessary to cover the subject content.

During the conversion of its records to the UKMARC format, the British Library proceeded to upgrade its indexing process. However, the chain index generated from the eighteenth edition of *DDC* did not lend itself to automated techniques. Since a computer-produced subject index was needed for the *British National Bibliography*, a satisfactory replacement for the chain indexing had to be found.

In addition, there had been a growing dissatisfaction with the existing classification schemes because of their inability to handle the rising output of materials in all fields. In both print and nonprint, there was an increasing incidence of complex or multifaceted subjects and a rapid growth of new concepts. The Classification Research Group (CRG) of the British Library and other groups had been working on an improved approach to classification to address the information explosion.

The research efforts of CRG focused primarily on the principles of faceted classification developed by Ranganathan. After examining the subject matter in special fields, they concluded that something approaching a common set of principles was frequently applied during the construction of schemes covering the range of topics in the subject spectrum. Meanwhile, research on indexing had been evaluating the relative value of natural language versus controlled vocabularies in the retrieval of documents. One-to-one relationships between terms which exist in their natural grammatical sequence or syntax were compared to the artificial language in use in controlled vocabulary.

Experience with indexing methods has also led to the development of thesaural principles to relate concepts effectively. The thesauri that resulted were lists of alphabetical terms in accordance with the principles of synonymy (*Use* references), hierarchy (BROADER TERM, NARROWER TERM), and word association (RELATED TERM). The terms in a thesaurus could be precoordinated to make class descriptions as needed.

CRG never relinquished its aim of producing a classification system; instead, it applied the principles of modern classification theory to a new indexing system that would accommodate all types of concepts and compound subjects in both print and nonprint. In 1974, after three years of trial and experimentation, the chain indexing of the *BNB* was replaced by PRECIS to produce the subject index. PRECIS-based catalogs and indexes for other agencies have been produced by the British Library's Local Cataloguing Service of the British Library Automated Information Services. The PRECIS system has been used to generate specialized catalogs, such as the *British Education Index*, which has been produced by the British Library since 1976. Some British libraries have tried to produce in-house PRECIS indexes and catalogs with varying degrees of success. The *British National Film Catalogue* applied the PRECIS system to its catalog in 1985.

In 1972, the *Australian National Bibliography* was indexed by the PRECIS system. However, the use of PRECIS was discontinued in 1985 on the grounds that it was no longer cost-effective, even though a subject index based on LC subject headings would be less specific. The use of LC subject headings is widespread in Australia, and many of the Australian libraries have joined the Australian Bibliographic Network, which uses the Western Library Network package with its large database of American cataloging complete with LC subject heading data.

Some countries, including Denmark, Italy, Poland, India, and China, are actively studying PRECIS linguistically. The existing English language codes have been successfully adapted. When direct machine translation from one language to another is available, the database can be queried in different languages; responses will appear in the language specified.

PRECIS could thus become an international subject indexing system because it is designed to take into account the linguistic idiosyncracies of other languages.

The PRECIS system is particularly attractive to Canadian libraries because of its capability of producing bilingual indexes. The catalogs of the Public Archives and Film Canadiana, now produced by the National Library of Canada, are indexed by PRECIS in both French and English. In 1973, school librarian Audrey Taylor developed a PRECIS index for the school collection at Aurora High School. Her work has since been incorporated into a computerized network for Ontario school libraries.

Experimentation by the National Film Board of Canada in 1978 elicited interest in the PRECIS system in the United States. The National Film Board of Canada (NFBC) wanted a subject access system to describe media in its catalogs and to improve the scheduling of its media collection throughout Canada. In 1975, Professor Mary Dykstra of the Dalhousie University School of Library and Information Studies was invited to study the problem, and she recommended the PRECIS system. NFBC first produced a PRECIS index in its 1978 catalog for the North Atlantic region. In 1982, NFBC has produced a separate computer-generated PRECIS index for its films in the NFBC *Programming Guide* and catalogs. Its 1988 catalog includes both bibliographic records and a PRECIS index.

In the mid-1970s, NFBC developed a national computerized information system known as FORMAT for the distribution of Canadian audiovisual materials. The FORMAT database, indexed by PRECIS, was designed to interpret Canada to Canadians and others. The database contains more than 12,000 bibliographic records, including films, videos, filmstrips, and multimedia. As resources permit, other types of materials, such as television programs, stock shot collections, and photos, are being entered into the database. FORMAT is currently available online from NFBC offices in Canada and the United States. This database will be available on CD-ROM at a later date. NFBC is planning to widen its link with private industry, university, and public libraries as well as to provide direct access to Canadian homes.

The computerization of the NFBC media file has also permitted the production of custom catalogs for libraries in both French and English. FORMAT is accessible through the cataloging support system of the University of Toronto Library Automated System (UTLAS). SofTech Inc. has developed PC-PRECIS, a microcomputer package for the National Film Board of Canada. PC-PRECIS is used by NFBC to generate its subject indexes, and it is available for local production of PRECIS subject indexes.

The Library of Congress actively watched the implementation of the PRECIS system in many countries. LC conducted a feasibility study of the system in 1978. By the time LC had evaluated PRECIS, the MARC database was already well-established, with Library of Congress headings in the primary subject field. LC did not accept PRECIS as a viable system due primarily to the excessive cost of maintaining two subject indexing systems.

Philosophy and Purpose

The PRECIS system was designed to produce an alphabetical subject index to be displayed on paper, on microform, or at a computer terminal. The system was intended to take the drudgery out of the indexing process. After the indexer has completed the intellectual analysis, operational codes are assigned for computer manipulation of the data to generate entries and to select the appropriate cross references from the computerized thesaurus.

The guiding principles for the implementation of the system are described in a text by Derek Austin, *PRECIS, A Manual of Concept Analysis and Subject Indexing*, published by the Council of the British National Library in 1974. Derek Austin's years of experience teaching the system and his developmental work on PRECIS at the British Library led to improvements in the system which are reflected in the second edition of the manual he co-authored with Mary Dykstra in 1984.

Austin, in the second edition of the official PRECIS manual, stated that PRECIS is not a subject heading system, although it can be used to organize entries in an alphabetic subject catalog in much the same way as traditional subject headings.[1] The terms in a PRECIS index are context-dependent on each other in contrast to the independent nature of terms in a subject heading system. Austin indicated that PRECIS uses a kind of indexing "grammar" to ensure that terms are organized consistently in meaningful sequences.

The PRECIS system has an open-ended vocabulary—that is, it allows the use of any natural language term to describe an item. The terms selected in PRECIS are as specific as the document requires, and references can be made to the broader concepts in the hierarchy. The order of terms in chain indexing must reflect the classification scheme and may appear somewhat unnatural when applied to a specific item. The filing order of terms is dictated by the function ascribed to each term. The citation order maintains the context-dependency of the elements in the string.

In 1981, Phyllis Richmond, professor of library science, Case Western Reserve University, adapted the official PRECIS manual to incorporate North American terminology "to allow PRECIS to stand on its own merits."[2] In 1985, Mary Dykstra produced *PRECIS: A Primer* to provide further guidance in the application of the system.

Austin's definition of PRECIS summarizes the system as having "two interrelating sets of working procedures.... The first refers to the organization of terms in input strings and their manipulation into entries... we might call this the syntactical side of the system."[3] The second set of procedures deals with the thesaural relationships between indexing terms and their synonyms, broader terms, and narrower terms. At the International PRECIS Workshop at the University of Maryland in 1976, Austin further expounded on the purpose of the PRECIS system.[4] He indicated that the system is based on a set of logical principles which can be applied consistently throughout the system and which provide a systematic way of analyzing the subject in terms of a faceting process that seeks to identify the object, the action, and the agent.

ORGANIZATION OF PRECIS

The process of describing the subject content of materials in PRECIS involves several activities. First, the indexer conducts a formalized examination of the document to describe the subject in a summary phrase called a subject statement or string. Then the indexer answers standard queries, such as what happened, when, where, who, or what did it, and why. By means of syntactical rules, PRECIS suggests a proper order of descriptive terms so each index entry is patterned logically on those preceding it. PRECIS favors passive grammatical structure for its subsequent ordering of terms, so that the object affected precedes the action itself, with the agent of the action following both. Next the indexer identifies any hierarchical relationships between the concepts. *See* and *See also* references are extracted from the machine-based thesaurus. These cross references have been replaced by *Search under* and *Related terms* respectively in the 1988 *Film and Video Catalogue* of the National Film Board of Canada.

When the function of each term is identified, operator codes are assigned to establish term order, punctuation, inversion, and substitution. The schema of operators shown in figure 1 includes both the primary and secondary operators and concepts that require consideration:

For indexers who are not using a computer to manipulate the terms in the string, the operator codes can serve as a checklist of the different aspects of the subject that should be incorporated into the subject description.

The key concepts (operators 1, 2, and 3) are generally encountered in an input string. Every string must contain, at the least, a term with the prefix '1' or '2'. For example, an item on the management of American libraries can be identified by three terms with different functions. The *location of the action*, America, can be described more specifically as United States and is coded (0). The term 'management' describes *the result of an action* and is coded (2); *the institution acted upon*, libraries, is coded (1). The use of the operators regulates the filing order:

String: (0) United States
      (1) Libraries
      (2) Management

The coding also ensures that the terms are set down in a context-dependent order. When order is not prescribed, the meaning can be ambiguous. For example, "management of American libraries" and "American libraries of management" have different meanings, and the computer could not order the terms without adequate direction.

Primary Operators

Environment of core concepts:	0	Location
Core concepts:	1	Key System Thing when action not present; thing towards which an action is directed, e.g. object of transitive action, performance of intransitive action
	2	Action; effect of action
	3	Performer of transitive action (instrument); intake; factor agent
Extra-core concepts:	4	Viewpoint-as-a-form; aspect
	5	Selected instance, e.g. study region; sample population
	6	Form of document; target user

Secondary Concepts

Coordinate concepts:	f	'Bound' coordinate concept
	g	Standard coordinate concept
Dependent elements:	p	Part; Property
	q	Member of quasi-generic group
	4	Assembly
Special classes of action:	s	Role definer; directional property
	t	Author-attributed association
	u	Two-way interaction

Source: Mary Dykstra, *PRECIS: A Primer* (Metuchen, N.J.: Scarecrow Press, 1987), 181.

Figure 1. Schema of operators.

It is the computer's job (although this tedious task can be done manually) to shunt the terms of an input string to generate entries for the subject index. The PRECIS manual explains the shunting process thus:

> we need to visualize the three parts of a PRECIS entry as positions in a railway yard, and imagine that a string of index term [sic], in input order, is marshalled in the display position ready for shunting.[5]

In a PRECIS index, each entry is displayed on two lines. The LEAD, or first, entry point and its QUALIFIER are included on the first line. The DISPLAY, indented on the second line, adds specificity to the LEAD:

Output   **UNITED STATES**   **(LEAD)**
                  Libraries. Management.   (Display)

Another entry for the item is produced as follows:

1. To generate the entry under "libraries," shunt this term to the LEAD position. The term United States becomes the QUALIFIER and is moved to the right of the new LEAD:

Output   LIBRARIES. United States
                  Management

2. To put the next term in the LEAD position, the process is repeated:

Output   MANAGEMENT. Libraries. United States

In each of the strings which contain an AGENT (code 3), and especially in those with both an AGENT and an OBJECT, the thing which functions as AGENT and OBJECT is connected to the central action by means of prepositions. Through predicate transformation, the computer can manipulate a string in PRECIS to produce entries in which the clarity of the relationships between ACTION, OBJECT, and AGENT is maintained in all permutations, as in the following example:

        String: (1) fiction
                            (2) reading $v by $w of
                            (3) children

        Output: FICTION
                            Reading by children

                            READING. Fiction
                            By children

                            CHILDREN
                            Reading of fiction

The PRECIS system also uses primary operators which describe some unique functions. Terms coded (4) can be identified by their focal nouns, including VIEWPOINTS for classes of people, PERSPECTIVES related to disciplines, or ASPECTS identifying the facets of the core concept. The following example illustrates the use of this operator (4) and the output generated by the computer:

>   Subject: Christian viewpoints on marriage
>
>   String: (2) marriage
>   (4) Christian viewpoints
>
>   Output: MARRIAGE
>   Christian viewpoints
>
>   CHRISTIAN VIEWPOINTS
>   Marriage

Operator (5) is used when the author features a general subject but cites a particular reference under one of the following categories: STUDY EXAMPLE, STUDY REGION, SAMPLE POPULATION, or SOURCE OF EVIDENCE. The following example shows how this operator is applied:

>   Subject: Unidentified flying objects in the Old Testament
>
>   String: (1) unidentified flying objects
>   (5) sources of evidence
>   (q) Bible. O.T.
>
>   Output: UNIDENTIFIED FLYING OBJECTS
>   —Sources of evidence: Bible. O.T.
>
>   BIBLE O.T. SOURCES OF EVIDENCE
>   Unidentified flying objects

The last of the primary operators supplies accessory information about the FORM of the document or the TARGET AUDIENCE. The next example shows how operator (6) is featured in the PRECIS system:

>   Subject: Sex roles in family life—an animated film for adolescents
>
>   String: (2) family life
>   (p) sex roles
>   (6) adolescents $01 for
>   (6) animated films
>
>   Output: FAMILY LIFE
>   Sex roles—For adolescents—Animated films
>
>   SEX ROLES. Family Life
>   —For adolescents—Animated films

ADOLESCENTS
    Family life. Sex roles—For adolescents
    —Animated films

ANIMATED FILMS
    Family life. sex roles—For adolescents

PRECIS allows the assignment of as many terms as are needed to describe the item. The system also requires the use of a code preceded by a dollar sign ($) to permit the addition of the word "for" to improve the meaning within entries.

It is possible with the PRECIS system to make reference to a subject which contains two or more coordinate subjects within a theme. The operator (g) in the following example leads to an entry which is a coordinate block as well as to individual entries:

    Subject: Design of engines and wings of aircraft

    String: (1) aircraft
                 (p) engines $v &
                 (g) wings   (Coordinate Block)
                 (2) design

    Output: AIRCRAFT
                  Engines & wings. Design

                ENGINES. Aircraft
                Design

                WINGS. Aircraft
                Design

                DESIGN. Engines & Wings. Aircraft

Use of the connectives $v and & will create a coordinate block. Note that when the terms in the coordinate block appear in the LEAD, the block is automatically suppressed from the entry. To prevent such suppression, the indexer uses the standard coordinate operator (f):

    Subject: Mixed flocks of ducks and geese in Canada

    String: (0) Canada
                 (1) ducks $v &
                 (f) geese
                 (r) mixed flocks

    Output: CANADA
                Ducks & geese. Mixed flocks

DUCKS. Canada
  Ducks & geese. Mixed flocks

GEESE. Canada
  Ducks & geese. Mixed flocks

If both of the coordinate elements were not included in the entries, the reference to mixed flocks would be confusing. This example shows the value of providing complete subject information at each entry point.

Three secondary operators focus on dependency. Operator (p) shows the relationship between the parts and the whole. According to the rule of differencing in PRECIS, a compound term like "camera lenses" has to be factored into separate entities, the focus being the lenses and the difference being the camera. The following string and resultant entries illustrates this point:

String: (1) cameras
          (p) lenses

Output: CAMERAS
          Lenses

          LENSES. CAMERA

In PRECIS, concepts relating to genus and species are effectively handled by *See also* or *Related terms* references. However, relationships such as between specific classes, such as mice, and broad classes, such as pests or pets, are only valid in certain circumstances. Such quasi-generic relationships are identified by operator (d), as in the following example:

Subject: Control of ants as pests

String: (1) pests
          (q) ants
          (2) control

Output: PESTS
            Ants. Control

          ANTS. Pests
            Control

Proper names or classes of a proper name may be subject terms; any specific person or corporate body may be a subject. The operator (q) is used to eliminate *See also* references in such instances:

Subject: Halley's Comet

String: (1) comets
          (q) Halley's Comet

Output: COMETS
          Halley's Comet

          HALLEY'S COMET

Another operator to describe dependency is operator (r), which is used to identify aggregates and associates, as in the following examples:

Subject: Behavior of elephant herds

String: (1) elephants
          (r) herds
          (sub 2) (1) elephant herds
          (2) behavior

Output: ELEPHANTS
          Herds. Behavior

          BEHAVIOR. Elephant herds

Subject: The wives of Henry VIII

String: (1) Henry VIII $f King of England
          (r) wives

Output: HENRY VIII, KING OF ENGLAND
          Wives

          WIVES. Henry VIII, King of England

The list of operators and codes that carry instructions to the computer is fundamental to the string-writing process. In PRECIS, manipulation codes provide machine-readable instructions for the generation of entries. The primary codes are assigned to designate links between terms in a coordinate theme or to distinguish between common and proper nouns. These codes are responsible for housekeeping functions:

Primary Codes
  Theme
  interlinks: $x 1st concept in coordinate theme
                 $y 2nd/subsequent concept in theme
                 $z Common concept

  Term codes
  also used in
  the thesaurus: $a Common noun
                 $c Proper name (class-of-one)
                 $d Proper name

Some documents cover two or more distinct topics. These coordinating themes are expressed in a single string by the theme interlink codes:

Subject:	Beekeeping and the marketing of honey in Nova Scotia	
String:	(z)(0) Nova Scotia	(Common Element)
	(x)(2) beekeeping	(Element of Theme 1)
	(x)(1) honey	(Element of Theme 2)
	(y)(2) marketing	(Element of Theme 2)
Output:	NOVA SCOTIA	
	Beekeeping	
	HONEY. Marketing	
	BEEKEEPING. Nova Scotia	
	MARKETING. Honey. Nova Scotia	

The secondary codes focus on differencing elements, either addressing a preceding, a parenthetical or a date difference. Computer instructions are embedded in a nine-position code assigned to an item by the indexer to guide the production of a computerized catalog.

Secondary Codes	
Differences	
(preceding):	$0 Non-lead, space generating
	$1 Non-lead, close up
	$2 Lead, space generating
	$3 Lead, closeup
Date as a difference:	$d
Parenthetical differences:	$n Non-lead parenthetical difference
	$o Lead parenthetical difference
	$v Downward-reading connective
	$w Upward-reading connective

Codes in PRECIS inform the computer about the nature of certain qualifying terms: ($a) for common nouns, ($c) for proper names, and ($d) for place names. These codes can be replaced by typographical codes that will govern the type style and punctuation.

Terms in PRECIS always are written in their natural language order. Inverted headings are not used in this system. However, the indexer can provide access to any of the words in a compound term by the technique of differencing. All strings include a focus, which is always expressed as a noun. The focal nouns can be accompanied by one or more differences, which are attributes that are possessed by some members of that focal class. There are two types of differences, preceding differences as in CHILDREN'S FILMS and following differences as in GAMES FOR CHILDREN. The rules of differencing guide the indexer in the factoring of compound subjects and tend to increase the level of consistency in the form of the headings. A numbered code is used to inform the computer whether to put all the differences in a LEAD position, as in the following two different examples:

Subject: Quick-frozen peas

String: (1) peas $21 frozen $32 quick-

Output: PEAS
       Quick-frozen peas

FROZEN PEAS
       Quick-frozen peas

QUICK-FROZEN PEAS

Subject: Partially skimmed milk

String: (1) milk $21 skimmed $02 partially

Output: MILK
       Partially skimmed milk

SKIMMED MILK
       Partially skimmed milk

Preceding differences are coded to generate appropriate headings:

Subject: Hospitals for children

String: Hospitals $21 children for

Output: CHILDREN
       Hospitals for children

HOSPITALS FOR CHILDREN

Dates are included in the string as a difference by the code $d. They can be added in either of two forms, i.e., "1945-" and "To 1775."

Parenthetical differences can also be added to the string, using the code ($n) for non-LEAD entries and the code ($O) for LEAD entries. An example of the latter follows:

Subject: Intelligence of infants as measured by the Wechsler scale

String: (1) infants
(p) intelligence
$0 Wechsler Scale

Output: INFANTS
          Intelligence (Wechsler Scale)

          INTELLIGENCE (Wechsler scale). Infants

          WECHSLER SCALE. Intelligence. Infants

PRECIS has a mechanism to permit several terms to appear both as units and as separate terms:

Subject: The planning of agricultural research

String: (2) agriculture
           (p) research   (sub 2) (2) agricultural research
           (2) planning

Output: AGRICULTURE
           Research. Planning

           PLANNING. Agricultural research

Typographic codes can also be added by the indexer to identify the typeface of filing and non-filing words:

$e: Non-filing part in italic preceded by comma
$f: Filing part in italic preceded by comma
$g: Filing part in roman, no preceding punctuation
$h: Filing part in italic preceded by full point
$i: Filing part in italic, no preceding punctuation

The last decision in the first phase of indexing in the PRECIS system requires the identification of those terms that will be given a lead position in the index. A checkmark is placed over these items. The computer will interfile the headings and alphabetically organize those with common LEADS so that the display line of the entries will function as subdivisions:

Output: UNITED STATES
          Libraries. Automation
          Libraries. Management

Vocabulary control is achieved by entering all terms used as LEAD terms in the thesaurus. Synonymous terms and other related terms which are not used are also included in the thesaurus because they function as users' points of access. The computer will generate the needed cross references automatically from the online thesaurus. *See references* in the PRECIS system direct the user to the synonym preferred by the system. This type of reference occupies one line in the index.

Character   *See* PERSONALITY

See also references, which occupy several lines in the index, join related terms in use in the 1981 index of the National Film Board of Canada.

AIR
See also
ATMOSPHERE
WIND

Thesaural relationships between terms are also indicated by special coding. There are three types of relationships that are recognized in the PRECIS system in accordance with the *Guidelines for the Establishment of Monolingual Thesauri*. The terms in the input strings are analyzed and described in terms of the following thesaural relationships in a PRECIS index:

1. Equivalence Relationship (code $m):
    a. Synonyms
        Birds/Aves
    b. Quasi-synonyms
        Hardness/Softness
2. Hierarchical Relationship (code $o):
    a. Generic relationship
        Rodents
        Mice
        Rats
    b. Whole/part Relationships
        1. Geographical regions
            United States
            California
            Los Angeles
        2. Systems and Organs of the Body
            Circulatory System
            Vascular System
            Arteries
        3. Areas of Discourse
            Science
            Biology
            Botany
    c. Associative Relationships (code $n):
        Birds/Ornithology
        Teeth/Dentistry

Equivalence relationships are identified when two or more terms are seen as expressing the same concepts for indexing purposes. Hierarchical relationships represent the most important relationship in thesauri, because they organize terms into structured sequences. Associative relationships provide links between terms which are not equivalent or hierarchical in nature, but the associations between them are sufficiently strong to justify a reference from one to the other in the index. Since the video terms were selected in accordance with established guidelines for thesaurus development, the National Film Board of Canada was able to substitute the preferred terminology for its 1988 index:

Character	Air
Search under	*Related terms*
PERSONALITY	WIND

Semantic relationships are provided through the syndetic structure of the PRECIS system. This mechanism has been invaluable to guide the user from a non-used, broader, narrower, or related term to the vocabulary in use by the system to describe the subject matter of a film or video.

Overall, the PRECIS system provides extensive guidance in the identification and organization of subject entries, with specific emphasis on the syntactical and syndetic relationships between terms in the headings assigned.

ANALYSIS OF INDEX

The PRECIS index generated by the National Film Board of Canada for the sample of one hundred films under study was compared to the two other indexes: the LC index and the NICEM index. These indexes were examined to ascertain the number of access points, the forms and types of headings assigned, the specificity of the headings, and the syndetic structure incorporated in the index. This analysis was conducted to identify the strengths and weaknesses of PRECIS. It is interesting to note that this index was designed not only for the rental and sales catalogs of NFBC, but also for use in the distribution of film and other media throughout Canada.

Vocabulary

Access Points. The indexing of each film as assigned by NFBC was examined to isolate the access points. The index was comprised of two types of access points, subject headings, which provide instant information, and cross references, which serve as links to other access points in the index. The PRECIS index included a total of 278 headings to describe the films in the study; this represented an average of 2.78 headings for each film.

When the cross references were considered, the access points increased 204 percent, to 8.60 for each film. PRECIS indexing included more cross references than LC and NICEM (LC: 1.52 headings a film, 2.56 cross references a film, with a 160 percent increase; NICEM: 3.78 headings a film, 3.23 cross references a film, with an 85 percent increase).

In addition to counting the number of access points, Maron's formulas for measuring exhaustivity were calculated to identify the depth of indexing and to determine the average term breadth.[6] The formulas were applied to all of the PRECIS headings generated by the manipulation of terms in the strings. Even non-LEAD terms were analyzed in the PRECIS index because the comparative analysis included many non-LEAD terms in the other two systems that would become access points in keyword searching. However, those phrases added by the indexer to clarify the meaning of the string (including "Attitudes of," "Use of," and "Role of") were not included in the count. Also excluded were defining words or phrases followed by a colon, such as "CHARACTERISTICS", and "SPECIAL THEMES:". The inclusion of these terms from the PRECIS string would unrealistically inflate the number of access points.

The depth of indexing was calculated by dividing the total number of headings by the total number of films. The depth of PRECIS indexing resulted in the assignment of 2.78 terms for each film; however, when non-LEAD terms were included in the count, the number increased to 3.60 terms a film. This compared to 1.52 terms a film for LC (1.95 terms a film when subdivisions and comma phrases were included), and 3.78 terms a film for NICEM (9.62 terms for each film when both the general topical headings and the subdivisions were included in the tally).

There was no direct correlation between the number of headings assigned by a system and its effectiveness in retrieval because it is the amount of subject information within headings that is important in the retrieval process. Therefore, the breadth of the indexing was calculated by dividing the total number of terms assigned by the PRECIS system by the total number of different terms in use. The PRECIS indexers assigned 205 different terms to the films, resulting in a term breadth of 1.35. When non-LEAD terms were included in the calculation, the indexing system had used 264 different terms with a term breadth of 1.36. The calculation of the breadth of indexing for the comparative indexes yielded 125 different terms and an indexing breadth of 1.21, or, including non-LEAD terms, 168 different terms and an indexing breadth of 1.16 for LC, 221 different terms and an indexing breadth of 1.71, or, including non-LEAD terms, 450 terms and an indexing term breadth of 2.13 for NICEM. NICEM provided more headings for each film and also included more and different terms to describe the films under study. However, more films were linked together in the PRECIS index. The links created between terms in the NICEM index were too general to allow precision in searching. The LC index was not as effective as the PRECIS index in linking films because the term breadth was automatically reduced by LC's limited cataloging policy. By providing comprehensive coverage of the content with the assignment of unique terms, the PRECIS indexers established more relationships between the films in the sample than the other two systems under study.

Terminology. PRECIS and LC frequently used similar words to describe films. For example, PRECIS used INTERPERSONAL RELATIONSHIPS; LC selected the shorter INTERPERSONAL RELATIONS. LC used the inverted

TALES, GHANIAN, while PRECIS assigned GHANA—FOLK TALES. The PRECIS and NICEM indexes did not share many synonymous terms, in part because the latter did not use terms from established subject heading lists.

The vocabulary used in the PRECIS index is open-ended, and new terms encountered in an item can be added to the vocabulary. Since this author did not view the films under study, she is not able to report on the use of terms in the index that reflected the soundtrack of the films. Instead, the study focused on comparing the terms assigned by the three indexes against terms in the thesaurus of the Hennepin County Public Library.

Both the Hennepin media catalog and the PRECIS index introduced the modern concept of endangered species in the headings RARE AND ENDANGERED ANIMALS and ENDANGERED SPECIES respectively. The sociological term AMERINDIAN CHILDREN was used in the Hennepin catalog, while the PRECIS index used INDIANS OF NORTH AMERICA—CHILDREN. PRECIS indexers assigned the term DOODLERS for *The Doodle Film*, while the Hennepin indexers applied the term SCRIBBLES AND SCRIBBLING. The Hennepin indexers agreed with the PRECIS indexers on the use of the heading TABLE MANNERS, as opposed to LC's TABLE ETIQUETTE.

Both the PRECIS index and the Hennepin media catalog assigned the term FILM instead of the synonyms MOVING PICTURES, MOTION PICTURES and MOVIES. The Hennepin index was more creative in its headings for filmic concepts than the PRECIS indexers; Hennepin adopted such terms as CINEMATIC POETRY, STORY WITHOUT WORDS, AMERICAN FILM FESTIVAL AWARD WINNERS and SATIRICAL FILMS. COMPUTER-ASSISTED ANIMATED FILMS was the assigned heading in the PRECIS index, while the Hennepin indexers assigned the term COMPUTER DRAWING.

Syndetic Structure. The PRECIS index revealed an intricate syndetic system to interrelate the assigned strings. Each LEAD term in the index was semantically related to other terms in the index. Once a term was established, cross references were generated automatically by the system. The fifteen *See* references in the PRECIS index were generated from terms that would have been likely access points. While the LC index had many more *See* references, the frequency of these references was not significant because they were often linked to terms that are not commonly used in communication.

The index included 111 *See also* references. A large number of these references emphasized the genus/species or part/whole relationships, in part because the PRECIS system requires the indexer to review and identify such relationships by code. A general *See also* reference linked SPORTS to specific sports and to narrower terms such as WINTER SPORTS and WATER SPORTS. The names of Indian tribes featured in the films were related to INDIANS OF NORTH AMERICA by a *See also* reference. VALLEYS *See also* OKANAGA VALLEY is representative of location headings used for cities, oceans, rivers, mountains, and national parks. Only twelve cross-categorical associations were found among the *See also* references, including relationships such as VIOLENCE *See also* WAR and FAMINE *See also* STARVATION.

Content Description

Specificity. Through its differencing rules, the PRECIS system permitted the generation of both general and specific entries from the assigned strings. For one of the films in the sample, there were entries under both WORKING MOTHERS and MOTHERS in the PRECIS index. Under the NICEM system, films are assigned either a general or a specific heading, but not both. LC has begun to adopt the policy of dual entry, but the policy has not been applied consistently.

Classification words were sometimes included in the PRECIS string for clarity. For the film *Blake*, the heading PILOTS was included as a LEAD, and it also appeared in the string to designate a class of people: PILOTS: BLAKE, JAMES. This technique was used eleven times in the PRECIS index.

Facet analysis, as defined by Vickery, was employed to separate the elements of the headings in each of the three indexes into comparable units.[7] The PRECIS system assigned more facets for each film than the other systems under review. The PRECIS index made reference to curriculum only when a discipline was a subject; only two films were thus described. *A is for Architecture* is a film about the history of architecture; the name of the discipline matched the heading. For the film *Alphabet*, PRECIS created the specific heading ENGLISH LANGUAGE. Alphabet. The PRECIS indexers were also unique in assigning the heading ENGLISH AS A SECOND LANGUAGE for the film *Drylanders*.

The TIME facet was significant only in the PRECIS index. This particular facet was used rather frequently in PRECIS, but not in the lead position. PRECIS differentiated between a full time span and a partial one. The subdivision —To 1954 was assigned to emphasize the historical perspective of *A Is for Architecture*. In the PRECIS index, specific dates were often added to the headings to describe specific events, including a sculpture symposium, the highlights of a hockey season, or a bicycle race.

The PRECIS system was also unique in its identification of space relationships. NFBC was interested in identifying films about Canada and films produced in Canada. Thirty-eight such references were made in the PRECIS index for the sample films—many more than were produced by either of the other systems. The PRECIS indexers assigned both general and specific headings in the SPACE facet in the film index. ALBERTA, BANFF NATIONAL PARK, and JASPER NATIONAL PARK were assigned for the film *Bighorn*; KLONDIKE GOLD RUSH, YUKON TERRITORY, and DAWSON CITY were assigned for the film *City of Gold*. For the film *Adelaide Village*, the PRECIS indexers added the non-LEAD explanatory phrase SPECIAL SUBJECTS: BAHAMAS to the specific heading VILLAGES. Terms other than geographic were also used to designate location. Words like CEMETERY, SPACE, and GOLD FIELDS identified a location for the action of the film.

The DESCRIPTOR facet in the PRECIS system was an important determinant of specificity. Substance, product, or organism made up the terms in this facet. PRECIS always assigned two LEAD entries for joint concepts like matter and energy. Adjectival phrases were frequently used in the DESCRIPTOR facet to add specificity. WORKING MOTHERS and MOTHERS provided both a general and a specific heading for a film. Headings such as PAS DE DEUX ADAGIO and CLASSICAL BALLET were much more specific than the headings used by the other systems. These headings were also linked to DANCING by a *See also* reference. The PRECIS indexers paid close attention to hierarchical relationships, and this served to link many films in the index. Part/whole relationships were used in the PRECIS index. Separate headings were generated in PRECIS for MINING and GOLD, MERRY-GO-ROUND and HORSES, and FEATHERS and BIRDS.

Fifty-five films in the sample were assigned the ACTION facet. A comparison of the action words used in the three indexes revealed different levels of specificity, as with the DESCRIPTOR facet. The most significant difference in specificity among the systems resulted from the assignment of both DESCRIPTOR and ACTION facets to the input string to describe the films. In the PRECIS index, the concepts describing films were expressed in a sentence-like string of words with a verb in the passive voice as in MANAGEMENT OF LIBRARIES. The context-dependency feature was achieved by first determining the object of the action. All other elements had to relate to the key element. For example, the subject of one film involved the construction of a skyscraper in New York by Iroquois Indians from Canada. The ACTION facet was expressed by the noun equivalent of the verb with the term CONSTRUCTION.

The methodology of PRECIS string-building appeared to encourage the use of the AGENT facet, since the names of veterinarians, authors, and a pilot were added to the strings although not all of the terms were put in the LEAD position. BLUEJAYS was the agent in the action of GREED for the film *The Hoarder*. The AGENT in PRECIS was often accompanied by a phrase describing the role of that agent: INFLUENCES OF MEDIA, ATTITUDES OF CORPORATIONS, CARVINGS BY HAIDA INDIANS, and THE ROLE OF CITIZENS. These phrases did not appear in the LEAD position; they were included only to improve the message.

The PRECIS indexers used subdivisions to express the VIEWPOINT of a film on a particular subject. In the film *Boo Hoo*, the phrase CARETAKER'S PERSPECTIVE was put in the LEAD position. In other instances, a phrase was included for information even though the phrase did not appear as the LEAD. Some of the phrases in the PRECIS strings showed relationships between elements in a most unusual way. Dual phrases were added in one film *Nell and Fred*: VIEWS OF OLD PEOPLE and VIEWS ON SENIOR CITIZENS' HOMES; however, neither of the phrases was a LEAD entry.

In the 1988 index of its films and videos, the National Film Board of Canada supplemented the PRECIS index with a broad category subject index that is primarily curriculum based.

Types of Headings. Special consideration was given by the PRECIS system for cinematic properties. Reality can be created or reported on film. Early films by Thomas Edison viewed events with the camera functioning solely as a recording device. Later, scenes were staged so the camera would describe the action more graphically.

Trick photography was needed to get the violin to shrink, grow and split in the film *Monsieur Pointu*. The slow motion in *Ballet Adagio* heightened the appreciation of classical ballet and permitted observation of the adagio movements in slow motion. Thirty-six films were assigned the standardized heading ANIMATED FILMS, and four films were assigned the heading EXPERIMENTAL FILMS. In addition to assigning headings for animation, information about technique was supplied. The heading WOODEN PUPPETS was supplied for the film *Spinnolio*, and COMPUTER-ASSISTED ANIMATION FILMS was assigned to the film *Hunger*.

In the PRECIS index, fifty films were assigned both topical and nontopical headings. While the film *The Lion and the Mouse* was the only fictional film without a topical heading, it was assigned four form headings that highlighted its literary and filmic qualities, AESOP, ANCIENT GREEK FABLE, ANIMATED FILMS and CHILDREN'S FILMS. Surprisingly, a few films had these headings as non-LEAD subdivisions. The indexers of the three systems assigned more topical than nontopical headings. However, PRECIS indexers included 59 nontopical headings in contrast to 14 for LC and 24 for NICEM. Sixty-six films were assigned both types of headings under the PRECIS system, while NICEM used both types of headings in 29 films and LC used both types for 11 films. Just one film was assigned only nontopical headings in the PRECIS index, but LC assigned only nontopical headings to 20 films and NICEM assigned only nontopical headings to 11 films.

Literary genre headings were used extensively as subdivisions in the PRECIS index. The heading BIOGRAPHIES linked three films. Short stories on film were grouped by country of origin under AMERICAN SHORT STORIES and CANADIAN SHORT STORIES IN ENGLISH. Myths and folktales were included as both general and specific headings: FOLK SONGS, SCOTTISH FOLKSONGS, MYTHS, or GREEK MYTHS.

Some non-LEAD genre subdivisions were used only once in the PRECIS index: —STORIES, —FOLK TALES, and —ALLEGORIES. Humor and satire were also cited as non-LEAD subdivisions: —SATIRICAL TREATMENT and —HUMOUROUS TREATMENT.

Certain films were uniquely described by the following subdivisions: —STUDY EXAMPLE:, —SPECIAL SUBJECT, and —SPECIAL THEME. In the film *The Hoarder*, the bluejay exhibits greed; this is described by the subdivision —CHARACTERISTICS: GREEK. Comparisons of two concepts were brought out in two ways. For the film *Cosmic Zoom*, the subdivision —COMPARATIVE STUDIES was used; in two other films, the concept was presented in a different form by the phrase COMPARED WITH.

>SOCIAL CONTROL
> Compared with the Crucifixion of Christ
>
>PEACE
> Compared with war

These non-LEAD phrases were added to enhance the subject description.

Structure of Headings

Form. Effective retrieval of films is often determined by the form of the headings, especially in manual indexes. The PRECIS system used more single-word headings, adjectival phrases, and subdivisions than either of the other two systems under study. This was due to the in-depth description given to each film by the system. As the PRECIS terms were rotated to the LEAD position, the additional entries that were created retained all the qualifying terms from the rest of the summary statement. In essence this system provides keyword searching in a manual indexing.

Sometimes it is not possible to express a concept by means of a single word. The PRECIS system used single-word terms extensively by assigning 149 single words in the LEAD position. All but 12 films were assigned at least one term with this form. In the PRECIS index, three films were assigned only a single-word heading, in sharp contrast to the usual practice of assigning the many terms that comprised the average PRECIS string in the index.

Some adjectival phrases were used to increase the specificity of headings in all three of the indexes. This practice by the systems was examined by comparing the structure of the assigned headings in the three indexes. The individual words in adjectival phrases were classified as being either DESCRIPTORS or SPECIFIERS, with the former representing the class and the latter representing the qualifying noun or adjective. The structural form of SPECIFIER DESCRIPTOR was used 51 times in the PRECIS index. Two other forms were used to a lesser extent; SPECIFIER SPECIFIER DESCRIPTOR was used seven times, and SPECIFIER'S DESCRIPTOR was used nine times.

The most common form of adjectival phrase in the PRECIS index was the two-word heading: a noun with a qualifying noun or adjective. In some of these headings, the first word was often the most important word, as in RESEARCH STATION, WEIGHT REDUCTION, VIOLIN PLAYING, WATER RESOURCES, MOUNTAIN REGIONS, and HAIDA INDIANS. When the second word was also important, two headings were created such as WAR TOYS and TOYS for the film *Toys*. The assignment of multiple entry points often resulted in both general and specific headings for a film.

In the PRECIS index, prepositional phrases were used only three times in the LEAD position, as illustrated by the following phrases: CANADIAN POETRY IN ENGLISH, ENGLISH AS A SECOND LANGUAGE, and STATES OF MATTER. Prepositions were introduced to add meaning, as in CARVINGS BY HAIDA INDIANS, and CONSTRUCTION BY IROQUOIS. Prepositional phrases such as ROLE OF, USE OF, VIEWS OF, and COMPARED WITH were used extensively in non-LEAD positions to clarify the meaning in the description of films.

Nontopical headings accounted for many of the adjectival phrases in use. Forty films were assigned the leading phrase ANIMATED FILMS, and nine films were listed under the possessive phrase CHILDREN'S FILMS. Ethnic, national, or geographic adjectives or nouns made the entries more specific. The term CANADIAN related many films on different aspects of Canadian society, such as CANADIAN INDIANS, CANADIAN PAINTINGS, or CANADIAN POETRY IN ENGLISH.

The PRECIS index had no conjunctive phrases as LEAD entries. However, such phrases were used four times in the strings: BANFF NATIONAL PARK AND JASPER NATIONAL PARK, FROGS AND MICE, and VETERINARIANS: DEMETRICK, VIC AND MAIDMENT, REG. No parenthetical phrases were used in the PRECIS film index.

The PRECIS index did not use inverted entries to relate headings, a common practice in the LC system. When the PRECIS indexer recognized the value of the inverted form, multiple headings appeared in the LEAD position. For example, the film *Matrioska* was assigned two lead entries, RUSSIAN DANCING DOLLS and DANCING DOLLS. The inclusion of the whole string with two LEAD entries permitted some sub-selection at each entry point in the index:

>DANCING DOLLS
>>Russian dancing dolls—Animated films
>
>RUSSIAN DANCING DOLLS
>>—Animated films

The PRECIS strings, which were often made up of phrases, were converted to single-word headings when terms were rotated to the LEAD position.

Similarities in the headings assigned by the PRECIS indexers and by indexers for the other two systems were examined. An exact match from all three systems was identified in only four headings for the 100 films. However, there was a match between the headings of the LC and PRECIS indexes in 33 instances. Sometimes the same words were included in headings in different ways by the three systems, or different words with the same root were used. Such "near matches" in headings were found in 76 headings assigned by LC and PRECIS. Interestingly, there was no match at all among the headings assigned by the three systems to 14 films. The PRECIS system requires that the string be written in the past tense; this resulted in greater consistency of form in the PRECIS index than in the other two systems.

Syntactic Relationships. In the PRECIS index, the shunting of terms to the LEAD position in the strings related the sample films under twenty-four terms. Five of these terms dealt with format: ANIMATED FILMS (37 films), BIOGRAPHIES (4 films), CANADIAN SHORT STORIES IN ENGLISH (2 films), EXPERIMENTAL FILMS (4 films), and LEGENDS (2 films). A number of non-LEAD filmic subdivisions were added to the PRECIS strings for the films under study: —FILMS INTERPRETATIONS, —FILM ADAPTATIONS, and —FILMS FOR TEACHING. Few films were related in the LC system. Many films in the NICEM index were related primarily through the assigned topical headings.

STRENGTHS AND WEAKNESSES

The PRECIS system was developed to replace the chain indexing mechanism in use for the *British National Bibliography* and to computer-generate an index in various formats: paper, microfiche, and online. After the adoption of the PRECIS system for the subject analysis of entries, *BNB* records became available in UKMARC format. The Library of Congress has been converting the MARC records of the British Library into USMARC format. Therefore, PRECIS headings for film and video are becoming available for adoption by bibliographic utilities. However, only UTLAS has loaded the NFBC films with the PRECIS strings into their system.

The 1988 PRECIS index for the National Film Board of Canada for the sample is included in the appendix to show not only the comprehensive treatment of subject description, but also the readable layout of the index.

Application Policies

Of the three systems under study, the PRECIS system offered the most guidance to the indexer by providing detailed rules and procedures to develop subject access points. The detailed indexing policy spelled out in the manual and guidebooks has tended to reduce inconsistencies in the assignment of headings.

The application of the PRECIS system is necessarily complex because it mirrors the complexity of the process of subject analysis. However, PRECIS has provided a systematic process of identifying the subject information in a comprehensive way. In addition, it has focused on the semantics and syntax of language to ensure good communication. Extra training may be required to take full advantage of the intricacies of this system. The PC-PRECIS software developed for NFBC helps to guide the indexer in applying the system. However, subject access to visual images requires in-depth analysis due to the nature of the medium and the need for accessibility to these resources.

Exhaustivity of Indexing

Access Points. The indexers using the PRECIS system are less constrained by established limits on the number of headings than the indexers using the LC system. The PRECIS indexers are required to think about content without regard to how the film and video could be used, while use is the primary consideration for indexing in the NICEM system.

PRECIS indexers focus on the subject content by identifying the subject matter in terms of core and extra core concepts. The schema of operators, designed to label the grammatical role of the terms in the input strings, serves as a checklist of concepts that can be considered for identification. The structured analysis in PRECIS indexing has guided indexers in providing comprehensive treatment of the subject content of all types of materials.

When comparing the subject indexes created under the guidelines of the three systems, the PRECIS index included the assignment of more of both topical and nontopical headings for films in the study. PRECIS included 205 different terms in the headings to describe the films, while the LC index had 125 unique words, and the NICEM index included 221 unique terms. Even though the NICEM index included a few more unique terms than the PRECIS index, the PRECIS terms were more specific and consequently were able to create better links between the films. The PRECIS terms were checked against an online thesaurus so that *See* and *See also* references could be generated automatically. Thesaural codes are being used in the 1988 PRECIS index instead of *See* and *See also* references and *Search under* and *Related terms* have replaced them. The checking was easily accomplished because PRECIS indexing is based on thesaural principles.

Terminology. The PRECIS vocabulary was much more current than were the terms assigned by LC or the curriculum-based NICEM system. Currency was determined by comparing the headings assigned by the three systems under review with the headings in the Hennepin County film catalog, which has always been cataloged under the most current terminology. There was more agreement between the headings in the Hennepin catalog and the PRECIS index than between the Hennepin catalog and either of the other systems.

PRECIS is based on an indexer-generated vocabulary. This open-ended vocabulary is a controlled language with an elaborate syndetic structure. This aspect of the system has made it especially suitable for media like films and videos, since new ideas often appear first in media.

Specificity. The PRECIS indexers described the sample films comprehensively by covering more of the facets identified by Vickery than the other two systems. The design of the PRECIS system produces both general and specific headings by the shunting of terms in the string to the entry position. Research has confirmed that users choose either general or specific headings when searching by subject. Therefore, assigning both types of headings, as has been done in the PRECIS index, is preferred. The assignment of multiple headings is especially important for items that cannot be browsed or that are available only on a rental basis.

Types of Headings. More films were assigned both topical and nontopical headings in the PRECIS index than in the other two indexes. However, the standardized nontopical terms list recently published by LC should be adopted by users of all systems to better describe the impact of style and technique on the message. Forty-three films were listed under ANIMATED FILMS in the PRECIS index. By including the whole string at each entry point, animal films that are animated can be quickly identified, as in the following example:

> **ANIMATED FILMS**
> Animals. Movement—*Children's films*
> **The Animal Movie.**
> Birds. Feathers—*Children's films*
> **Fine Feathers**
> Frogs & Mice—*Stories.*
> **Mr. Frog Went A Courting**

The description of a film under multiple LEAD terms permits much linking among the entries in an index.

Structure of Headings

There were more single-word access points for the sample films in the PRECIS index than in the other two indexes, and the single-word access points were displayed in the PRECIS index with all the terms in the string at each entry point. In addition to adding information at each entry point, this approach provides a means of categorizing the films under each entry term.

The PRECIS system requires the use of natural language order in the subject description. While inverted headings are not permitted, the shunting of terms has resulted in the same classification effect without using an artificial form. The PRECIS rule of differencing has permitted complex descriptions to be factored into separate terms that can be related to each other through the syndetic structure. This feature has significantly increased the links between films in the PRECIS index.

The cost of adopting such a system is high. In addition to the high cost of implementation, the large number of entries for each item increases the cost of producing such an index. While PRECIS has been described as labor-intensive, it does provide comprehensive subject access points. Information retrieval is totally dependent on the comprehensiveness of the indexing process and the specificity of the headings or terms assigned. The indexing is not significantly improved when the information is available on computer.

PRECIS has made a major impact on the subject control of materials by introducing a systematic approach to identifying different aspects of a subject in films and videos. The strict attention to linguistic principles has also facilitated the translation of the PRECIS strings and output in different languages. The PRECIS system is ideally suited to describe media comprehensively and to ensure their effective retrieval.

Notes

1. Derek Austin and Mary Dykstra, *PRECIS: A Manual of Concept Analysis and Subject Indexing* (London: British Library, 1984), 2.
2. Phyllis Richmond, *Introduction to PRECIS for North American Usage* (Littleton, Colo.: Libraries Unlimited, 1981), 28.
3. Austin and Dykstra, *PRECIS*, iv.
4. Austin, quoted in Hans Wellisch, *The PRECIS Indexing System, Principles, Applications and Prospects: Proceedings of the International PRECIS Workshop. University of Maryland, Oct. 15–17, 1976* (New York: H. W. Wilson, 1977), 5.
5. Austin and Dykstra, *PRECIS*, 12.
6. M. E. Maron, "Depth of Indexing," *Journal of the American Society for Information Science* 30 (July 1979): 224.
7. Ibid.

CHAPTER

6
Alternatives in Subject Access

During the 1970s, the library community grappled with a myriad of problems caused by the automation of records and the sharing of records via bibliographic utilities. The form and content of bibliographic records, AACR2, and the design of online catalogs were important issues. During the 1980s, subject access to bibliographic records became the primary research focus, with emphasis on the logic, adequacy, and compatibility of indexing systems. The research on subject access systems was extended to specialized materials such as the film indexing study described in this book.

MEDIA COLLECTIONS

The selection of a subject access system for media collections requires a thorough understanding of the goals of the institution, with specific attention to the purposes of the collection, probable and potential uses by the collection's clientele, the uniqueness of the media, and accessibility to the collection by those whom the institution is dedicated to serve.

An index to a media collection should be organized to meet the varied and changing needs of patrons. Is the index sufficient for identifying media primarily in terms of curriculum when the collection is housed in a school? When films or videos are linked to specific curricular areas, does this organization discourage teachers in other disciplines from considering those media for use? Do patrons shy away from films that are linked to many different disciplines? Shouldn't the subject headings and indexing terms emphasize cinematic techniques and genre, especially when the mode of presentation controls the message? Shouldn't we consider the assigning of descriptors to important sequences, as the television industry does for its programming? Users have never requested the identification of sequences in a film or video, possibly because such information has not been available. Why hasn't the existing research on the subject analysis of visual collections been applied to media indexes? Such questions must be answered before the development and selection of a subject access system.

Alternatives in Subject Access   107

The purpose(s) of a media collection may require different levels of indexing. The indexer must identify the present and anticipated uses of the collection by examining the continuum of uses, ranging from research to recreation. A needs assessment can help determine the depth of indexing required. There should be enough available information to provide reasonable certainty about the content and value of a particular film or video.

How does one determine what kind of information will meet the needs of patrons? There is very little in the literature about how people view films or videos. Individuals and groups usually view a film from beginning to end, even though technology permits the user to "fast forward" the film or reverse the video to a particular sequence. Could it be that the law of "least effort" is at play and that the difficulty of identifying a film sequence on a topic or concept explains why this media information is not frequently used in documentation? Have we been supplying so little information about the content of films or videos that users have been required to view films or videos in their entirety? Why haven't film clips been used in much the same way as quotes from printed materials?

Computer and video technology may well modify the viewing and listening habits of users and create new and different demands on information retrieval systems. Heretofore, information from text, graphics, and moving images has been largely fragmented. Multimedia information can now be linked by computer to simulate the action of the human brain as it jumps from one related thought to another, following an intricate web of associative trails. Interactive hypermedia programs will be able to deliver information in a nontraditional manner by linking concepts from different electronic documents, including both text and graphics. Even the 1991 White House Conference on Library and Information Services planners have developed such a program to offer users information appropriate to their level of understanding, degree of interest, or time constraints. The Cleveland Public Library is subject searching its image database of one million photographs. Such new methods of using media require in-depth indexing to identify concepts and nontopical aspects of description. Films and videos need to be described both in a summary fashion and in terms of specific sequences when they become a mainstay in hypermedia programs.

ACCESS

Films and videos are very different media. Like video, film is a means of reproducing moving images; unlike video, it is a chemical rather than an electronic process. Film is still the medium of choice for group viewing and for capturing detailed images on the screen. Film projectors are not

108 Alternatives in Subject Access

usually owned by individuals, and viewing has been done mostly in public places. Since films have been chiefly produced and distributed by large media companies, film programming has been limited to what has been available in the marketplace.

Films have not been readily available because film collections have been largely centralized. The amount of information available about a specific item has been the critical factor in determining whether or not a film or video is rented or shared by institutions. Insufficient content information has meant that films requested for borrowing were often unusable. As a result, there has been a tendency to order only the tried and true films, and many appropriate selections have not been considered.

Video, an offshoot of television, has been a medium used for both commercial programming and local production. The independent video movement has explored this medium as a means of artistic creation and as an alternative for providing information. The availability of videocassette recorders in over half the homes in the United States has contributed significantly to the video revolution. More films have been transferred into the less expensive video format, and are finding their way into homes from either libraries or video stores.

Most video collections have the advantage of being housed locally. It is not uncommon for libraries to own 10,000-item video collections. Public libraries and video stores generally describe their holdings by displaying the video containers, which provide limited subject information—a picture and a marketing blurb intended for the prospective buyer. Videos in libraries have often been treated like bestsellers, with limited subject access. Most collections have been organized under broad categories.

Even when media collections are available locally, items on a specific subject cannot be easily identified. Some collections have been organized by accession numbers or stored in closed stacks. Patrons using videos stored in open stacks have been handicapped because the content was not readily identifiable by browsing. Films or videos cannot be previewed without equipment. No built-in indexes, such as a table of contents or back-of-the-book index, have been available to provide specific information about a film or video, let alone a specific scene within a video. Printed literature, which accompanies some items, often provides limited information. Surrogate records in media indexes have been the only means of providing intellectual access.

SUBJECT ACCESS

The efficiency of any media delivery system has been dependent primarily on the intellectual access to media in the form of cataloging and indexing terms in indexes or in the abstracts in bibliographic records.

Traditionally, subject access systems have been developed or selected by focusing on the predetermined body of knowledge requiring analysis. When films and videos first appeared on the scene, it seemed appropriate at the time to integrate these new media with existing print collections and to promote access in integrated catalogs or indexes. Some institutions, however, preferred to maintain separate catalogs and even developed subject access systems exclusively for media indexes.

The moving image in films and videos communicates someone else's perception of reality. Films and videos have required special treatment to adequately identify their subject content. The physical or literal description of media has been identified primarily by assigning controlled subject headings and indexing terms or by categorizing media under classed groups. The analysis and interpretation of moving images as secondary subject matter has been handled with limited coverage through the assignment of nontopical headings featuring genre, theme, or technique.

The assignment of subject headings and indexing terms has not only been dependent on the indexer's background and experience but also on his or her understanding of the visual image. Knowledge acquired through practical experience can be applied to describe images in terms of objects, events, or expressional qualities (primary subject matter.) However, the analysis and interpretation of images can only be made with a thorough knowledge and understanding of literary sources and film and video history. Film specialists can best provide this secondary subject matter.

Of the three systems under study, the NICEM index provided mostly primary subject matter through the assigned descriptors. The organization of this index into twenty-six curricular categories resembles the class groupings in many media catalogs. These discipline-based categories focus chiefly on the intended use of the film or video. Only the topical and nontopical subheadings provide content description at different levels of specificity.

The subject headings in the Library of Congress index have been drawn from a controlled vocabulary of both topical and nontopical headings, without reference to potential curricular usage. Generalized headings have not been assigned in the LC index unless specific headings did not exist or were not created. The specificity of the headings in the LC index has resulted in greater accuracy in the identification of primary subject matter than was possible in the NICEM index. The policy of LC indexers in limiting the number of headings for a film or video affects how much subject information will be available in the surrogate records.

By contrast, the PRECIS indexers provide greater access to primary subject matter by describing the content specifically and comprehensively. Curriculum information is not available in the index, because the indexing describes only content, not usage. PRECIS was adopted by the National Film Board of Canada to improve the dissemination of the media through its *Programming Guide*. Users have expressed great satisfaction with the PRECIS index when it was used for their media collections.

Abstracts

All three indexes in the study utilized the traditional approach of providing subject information by including subject headings or indexing terms and an abstract for each item. The abstracts in the three indexes described mostly primary subject matter. In-depth indexing of the primary subject matter could eliminate the need for abstracts by providing the information in a compact form and by using a controlled vocabulary. The size of each record could be reduced, but more importantly, the searching of subject headings and indexing terms would be much more cost-effective in the online environment. The efficiency of generating, storing, and retrieving abstracts should be reviewed, especially when abstracts include such a high ratio of non-information words to information-bearing words. The Oslo, Norway, library school opted to eliminate abstracts from its film catalog because of the superiority of the description of the films in its PRECIS index.[1] By adopting this practice, the cost of producing indexes could be reduced significantly without reducing the quality of the informational message of the primary subject matter.

The abstract and notes area could be reserved exclusively for the analysis and interpretation of films and videos by media specialists, who have the expertise to provide an in-depth analysis and to make references to the critiques of the media. There are two current sources of media information that address secondary matter effectively. The catalogs of the Museum of Modern Art have included secondary subject matter in essay form exclusively. The online version of *Magill's Survey of Cinema* in Dialog includes descriptors and an abstract for primary subject matter in the bibliographic records. The secondary subject matter is found in separate critical essays, which can be retrieved by free-text searching.

Searching Environment

More access points and lengthier abstracts have generally been available in online catalogs. The lack of specificity in the NICEM headings has been especially troublesome in the online environment, and users have been required to combine keywords to increase the precision of their searches. The retrieval capabilities of computer searching have not been optimized by LC's policy of limiting the number of access points for an item. Keyword searching and the post-coordination of terms can only be effective with adequate subject analysis. Interestingly, online mechanisms have simulated the shunting and coordination of terms that have been inherent features of the PRECIS system in both manual and online environments. The synthetic feature of the PRECIS system requires a precoordination into a summary statement of facets identified in the subject analysis. In addition, the user can still post-coordinate the same keywords online. The capability of precoordinating terms was found to be especially useful in social sciences subjects because terms have tended to be used less precisely and often overlap in meaning, and new terms are emerging. Therefore the comprehensiveness of the PRECIS string and the specificity of the terms within it have made this system equally effective in both the manual and the online environments.

Application Practices

Most of the information in the LC and NICEM abstracts and headings has been derived for publicity releases from producers or distributors. The practice of previewing media prior to indexing has been gaining favor. The producers of the media indexes for the National Film Board of Canada and the *Educational Film Video Locator* have both adopted this practice. While previewing has increased the cost of producing indexes, the identification of indexable concepts and the assignment of appropriate headings has improved markedly. The practice of assigning subject headings from secondary sources should be discontinued because there can be no guarantee that the subject information in the releases is adequate or accurate. If LC or NICEM are unable or unwilling to preview media during the indexing process, the indexing should be deferred to cooperating institutions. Previewing will be especially important in identifying those film and video sequences that should be indexed.

Over the years, indexers have been given limited guidance about how to examine and describe the content of an item. LC has required its indexers to summarize the subject content, no matter how complex, in an average of 1.5 headings for each film or video. The NICEM indexers have focused on relating subject content to potential uses by assigning media to as many discipline-based categories as applicable. The indexers at LC and NICEM need to examine their analysis protocol to improve the subject coverage of individual media items. The 1982 guidelines developed by the International Organization for Standardization in *Methods for Examining Documents Determining their Subjects and Selecting Indexing Terms* could be used. There should be a clear indexing policy that is consistently applied and clearly explained to the indexers and users alike.

The LC system needs to review its application policies with regard to media. LC should adopt some of the practices of the Hennepin County Public Library and incorporate the knowledge obtained from subject analysis research to significantly improve subject access to media. While the application policies of the NICEM system are adequate, there is a need both for greater specificity in the terms assigned and for a supporting syndetic structure. The NICEM index often does not include both topical and nontopical headings in the bibliographic records. Thus, users familiar with a particular title cannot go to a record for help in identifying other titles on the same subject.

By comparison, the PRECIS system employs a detailed and rigorous procedure on how to describe subject content. The role operators, fundamental to the string-writing process in PRECIS, are used to specify the grammatical function of the terms in a string. The list also serves as a checklist to systematically analyze subject content to insure comprehensive treatment of the subject matter.

EXHAUSTIVITY OF INDEXING

Access Points

Retrieval has been directly dependent on the number and type of headings assigned to describe subject content. There is usually a limit placed on access points in order to contain the processing effort and expense. For each access point in manual catalogs, a separate record must be generated and interfiled. While computerized records in the MARC format can accommodate more subject headings, LC has not significantly revised its policy of limited entries for all types of materials. Both NICEM and the NFBC have generated their records on computers to produce both their online databases and their hard copy indexes. Access points have been added to computerized records without significantly increasing the processing time and the storage requirement. This may explain in part why the NICEM and PRECIS indexes include more access points for each video or film.

Precision in retrieval has been more dependent on the subject content of each access point than on the number of access points assigned. Imprecise recall can increase processing time and requires more user effort. By assigning a limited number of specific headings, the LC index provides high precision but low recall. The vocabulary in the NICEM index includes a large number of compound headings of a general nature. This has resulted in high recall but low precision. The PRECIS index includes many of context-dependent specific descriptors, resulting in precise, efficient, and effective retrieval in both the manual and online environments.

The language of the LC headings is traditional and changes very slowly. The NICEM headings reflect the traditional curriculum rather than current topics featured in the media. The open-ended vocabulary of the PRE-

CIS system permits the assignment of current terminology. The currency of terms is important in describing media because media is often used to introduce new ideas, new products, and new applications.

Syndetic Structure

Users have been known to search under either general or specific headings during the retrieval process. Therefore, the existence of ancillary devices to help the user locate a desired item is important. In an index, the syndetic structure defines the term parameters, identifies the relationships among terms that are scattered throughout the index, or guides users to the preferred terms in the thesaurus. The decision to incorporate an elaborate syndetic structure into an index is often dependent on whether the index producers are willing to increase the processing costs or transfer the costs to users during the retrieval process. However, since many online systems are loading multiple thesauri on their systems and are resorting to automatic subject switching to improve subject access, indexes will require adequate thesauri.

Each of the three indexes under study was examined for the existence of a syndetic structure. The lack of an adequate syndetic structure in the NICEM index is a major flaw. If any enhancements for the NICEM index are projected, the systematic development of a syndetic structure should take priority. Such a process would require an unbundling of terms in the existing compound headings. Thesaural codes should replace the traditional *See* and *See also* references.

The syndetic structure in the Library of Congress system has also required some revamping. LC has already adopted thesaural codes with the eleventh edition of *LCSH*. However, this is only the first step in a major overhaul. The limitations of this alphabetically-based indexing system were apparent when the subject terms of some fields were arranged conceptually. The alphabetical list, with scope notes, applicable subdivisions, and nonused terms, must be supplemented by a hierarchical arrangement of terms to develop a system of broader and narrower terms. Some work has already been done in the art and architecture sections of LCSH and has culminated in the *Art and Architecture Thesaurus*. Using the MeSH list as a model and applying thesaural principles, both the vocabulary and the syndetic structure of LC subject headings for art and architecture have been significantly enhanced. In essence, LC subject headings can be structured hierarchically if experts within subject areas are assigned the task of examining the vocabulary in their fields. The inverted forms need to be changed to use only natural language. LC subject headings have to be reworked to separate the terms in compound headings and to make all nouns in the plural. By making a hierarchical list of the headings in *LCSH*, the missing links in the hierarchy can be corrected.

The PRECIS system was initially based on thesaural principles, and the adoption of thesaural codes was adopted in the 1988 index by NFBC. This index provides only two types of cross references, *Search under* and *Related terms*. The syndetic structure serves as a bridge between the language of the indexer and the user of the index.

Specificity of Indexing

For optimum retrieval, the index must describe the respective items both comprehensively and with sufficient specificity to uniquely describe a film and to relate this film to other films in the index. The analysis of media should rigorously systematize the identification of all concepts in the subject instead of focusing on developing a summary description. Facet analysis followed by synthesis encompasses the modern theory of subject analysis. The role operators developed by the PRECIS system could serve as a checklist to ensure that all aspects of a subject have been examined. Figure 2 shows how facet analysis can be coupled with specificity in terms to provide a comprehensive description of primary subject matter. The film *High Steel* describes the construction of a skyscraper in Manhattan by Iroquois Indians from Canada. The three systems under study analyzed this film very differently, as illustrated by the cataloging and indexing terms assigned.

Facet analysis is recommended in addition to the use of the *LC Thesaurus of Graphic Materials: Topical Terms for Subject Access*, a controlled vocabulary of 6,000 topical terms describing a broad range of subjects.

FACETS	NICEM (6)	PRECIS (5)	LC (2)
CURRICULUM	GEOGRAPHY INDUS. & TECH. EDUC. SOC. SCIENCE		
TIME		1960–69	
SPACE	CANADA	MANHATTAN NEW YORK	CAUGHNAWAGA RESERVE, QUE.
OBJECT		SKYSCRAPERS	
ACTION	CONSTRUCTION	CONSTRUCTION	
AGENT	INDIANS OF NORTH AMERICA	IROQUOIS	CAUGHNAWAGA INDIANS

Figure 2. Comparison of Facets

There has been great confusion about whether media should be described in terms of subject analysis or curricular orientation. Even though the need for exhaustive indexing for media has been recognized, many indexes have provided only general headings. Vendors will continue to use the general headings to market media by discipline. The "AV Forecast" section in *School Library Journal* has provided an alerting service in sixty-two categories, which includes both curricular areas and broad topics such as DRUGS AND ALCOHOL and SOCIAL STUDIES—MAP SKILLS. The 1989 edition of *Video Source Book* includes both a general category index, with eight major subject sections, and a subject index "with over 400 precise headings from 'abortion' to 'zoology'." In 1988 the *Media Review Digest* has organized media reviews under ninety subject headings and cross references. It is unfortunate that curricular description has been combined with subject information. A hierarchical structure is impossible with this mix because of the interdisciplinary nature of many media items. Curricular information is best provided separately from subject information. The 1988 NFBC catalog includes both a PRECIS index and a broad categories index.

Types of Headings

The treatment of nontopical aspects was inadequate in all the indexes, in part because a standardized list of subject headings was nonexistent until recently. Terms adopted in one reference tool were often not recognized in another. Anyone working with media should recognize the importance of adopting LC's new standardized procedures and nontopical headings, described in *Descriptive Terms for Graphic Materials: Genre and Physical Characteristics Headings*, and *Moving Images: Genre Terms*. The specificity of nontopical headings needs to increase in all systems. For example, LC has identified fifteen types of animated films; this information should be made available because the medium can truly affect the message.

Topography

The PRECIS system has been designed to provide an easy-to-read layout in the index. The terms in the output are context-dependent. The entries in the PRECIS index are displayed on two lines with the LEAD and its QUALIFIERS on the first line. The display is indented on the second line. The PRECIS layout can be examined in the appendix. The context-dependency of the terms in the entries has enabled indexers to generate multilingual indexes. In addition, the system has the unique feature of being able to shunt terms to the lead position, thereby generating multiple entry points. All terms in the string remain at each entry point for clarity.

The shunting of terms accords the classification provided by inverted headings without the disadvantages of the artificial form. The shunting of terms to entry positions in manual catalogs has also provided the advantage of access by keywords previously available only in online systems. The recently released PC-PRECIS, a state-of-the-art computer software package developed for the National Film Board of Canada by the engineers at Softech, Incorporated, will provide guidelines for the application of PRECIS for the local generation of media catalogs.

If one picture can speak a thousand words, we can well understand why it has been so difficult to produce an accurate description of subject content for moving images. The NICEM indexers were so preoccupied with linking films to the curriculum that their descriptions of topical and nontopical aspects were inadequate and inconsistent. In assigning subject headings for films and video, LC indexers focused on the important aspects of the works and were restricted to providing only indexing by summarization. The PRECIS system provides superior subject and vocabulary control for media. The "whole" subject, as defined in a PRECIS string, involves an enumerative synthetic and faceted process which applies the modern theory of subject analysis.

Our valuable media collections have been underutilized. Only adequate subject analysis can unleash the wealth of visual information in the moving image.

Note

1. Ole Gunnar Evensen, *PRECIS-basert Gjenfinningssystem for Kortfilm* (Oslo: Hovedoppgave ved Statens Bibliotekhogskole, 1980).

APPENDIX

A Sample PRECIS Index

The PRECIS system provides a set of procedures to translate the subject content of a film or video into syntactical entries and to relate the terms assigned to other terms which may occur to the user. While traditional indexes provide subject access by producing discrete headings, the PRECIS system yields a comprehensive description organized into a statement with different points of entry. Each entry point repeats the statement in different order. Each PRECIS entry is displayed on two lines. The LEAD, or first entry point, and its QUALIFIER are included on the first line. The DISPLAY, indented on the second line, adds another point of view to the LEAD term in addition to the categorization on the first line.

Entries in a Traditional Index:
AUDIOVISUAL MATERIALS
MOTIVATION (PSYCHOLOGY)
STUDENTS
TEACHING—AIDS AND DEVICES

Entries in a PRECIS Index:
AUDIOVISUAL AIDS. Schools
   Influence on motivation of students

MOTIVATION. Students. Schools
   Influence of audiovisual aids

SCHOOLS
   Students. Motivation. Influence of audiovisual aids

The following summary is necessarily brief and provides only an overview. For users who wish to apply the system, page references to the appropriate chapters in this book and in Mary Dykstra's *PRECIS: A Primer* are included for an explanation and elaboration of each step.

118   Appendix

1. *Subject Statement*
Generate a mini-abstract by completing the statement, "This film is about...." Because PRECIS consists of a set of procedures for subject analysis and not a vocabulary, the system can be adapted to different levels of specificity as needed.

The subject statement should read, "The film is about management of libraries in the United States."

Consult chapter 5 herein and Dykstra's *Primer,* chapters 2–6, pp. 8–108.

2. *Syntactic Analysis*
Analyze the statement to determine the functional role of each significant term by asking questions such as:

Did anything happen?
If yes, to whom or what did it happen?
Who or what did it?
Where did it happen?

This analysis permits the assignment of role operators for the above example.

The role operators would be assigned as follows:

management—**action**
libraries—**object of action**
United States—**location**

Consult list of operators in this book (chapter 5, p. 107+) and in Dykstra's book (chapters 7–12, pp. 109–78).

When the terms are assigned operator codes (number or letters) to describe role of the term in the statement, a PRECIS string will be generated:

(0) United States
(1) Libraries
(2) Management

Consult the list of operators in Chapter 5 of this book.

3. *Coding for Computer Storage*
Generate a nine-position code for the computer manipulation of the string to produce entries including format, with lead entries preceding punctuation and typography coding.

The computer code: $z11030$a Libraries

Explanation of code:
$ Indicator: start of primary code
(z) Instruction: single-theme string
(1) Instruction: operator (1)

(1) Instruction: lead the term
(0) Instruction: term is not a substitute
(3) Instruction: no special instructions for printing when not in lead
(0) Instruction: (presently unused)
($) Indicator: start of term code which determines secondary codes to follow
(a) Instruction: term is a common noun

Consult Dkystra's *Primer* (chapter 13, pp. 181-93).

4. Thesaural Relationships

The thesaural aspect of the PRECIS system involves a set of working procedures separate from the set of procedures for entry generation from the string. The process focuses on a priori relationships which are independent of the treatment of a concept in a particular film or video. Each term in use is assigned a Reference Indicator Number (RIN) which is a computer address in the PRECIS database to facilitate retrieval. In this network of addresses, data assigned to a specific address may easily be changed (e.g., Sri Lanka replacing Ceylon). Based on *The Guidelines for the Establishment of Monolingual Thesauri*, the PRECIS system seeks to identify three fundamental relationships between terms: equivalence, hierarchical, and associative. The thesaural network establishes the relationship between terms in the standard thesaural patterns to reveal broader terms (BT), narrower terms (NT), and related terms (RT) for each entry.

Consult Dykstra's *Primer* (chapter 14, pp. 196-208).

5. Subject Package

The indexer may wish to link the PRECIS description to classification numbers or other subject headings, either standard or local. This subject package is assigned a Subject Indicator Number (SIN). When another film or video is encountered on exactly the same subject, the indexer merely quotes the SIN to complete the processing.

Consult Dykstra's *Primer* (chapter 13, pp. 230+).

The following index was created from entries in the *National Film Board of Canada Film and Video Catalogue* (1988). The entries are used with permission of Audiovisual Services, National Film Board of Canada. The board is the major Canadian user of the PRECIS system.

ADAGIO. Classical ballet
   Pas-de-deux adagio –
    Experimental films
        Ballet Adagio.

ADOLESCENTS
   RELATED TERMS
   PUBERTY

ADVERTISING MEDIA
   Influence on girls' marriage expectations
    "...and They Lived Happily Ever After".

AESOP. Ancient Greek fables
   – *Animated films* – *Children's films*
    The Lion and the Mouse.

AGED PEOPLE
SEARCH UNDER
ELDERLY PEOPLE

AGGRESSION
RELATED TERMS
VIOLENCE

AIRCRAFT. Canada
Flying. James, Blake –
Biographies
                              Blake.

ALBERTA
Banff National Park & Jasper National Park. *Bighorn sheep – Life cycle*
                           Bighorn.

ALPHABETS. English language – *Children's films*
                           Alphabet.

ALPINE SKIING. Canada
Murray, Dave – *Biographies*
                           Descent.

AMERICAN FICTION
RELATED TERMS
AMERICAN SHORT STORIES

AMERICAN SHORT STORIES
White, E.B. – *Film adaptations – Animated films*
The Family That Dwelt Apart.

ANCIENT GREEK FABLES
Aesop – *Animated films – Children's films*
The Lion and the Mouse.

ANCIENT GREEK MYTHS
Characters: Icarus – *Film adaptations – Animated films*
                           Icarus.

ANIMALS
RELATED TERMS
ENDANGERED SPECIES
VETERINARIANS

ANIMALS
Movement – *Children's films – Animated films*
                        The Animal Movie.

ANIMATED FILMS
American short stories. White, E.B. – *Film adaptations*
The Family That Dwelt Apart.
Ancient Greek fables. Aesop – *Animated films – Children's films*
The Lion and the Mouse.
Ancient Greek myths. Characters: Icarus – *Film adaptations*
                           Icarus.
Animals. Movement – *Children's films*
                        The Animal Movie.
Beads
                           Bead Game.
Birds. Feathers – *Children's films*
                         Fine Feathers.
Bluejays. Characteristics: Greed – *Children's films*
                         The Hoarder.
Canada. Federalism
                   Propaganda Message.
Canada. Prison life
                           Prison.
Canadian Indians. Cultural identity
Charley Squash Goes to Town.
Canadian short stories in English. Richler, Mordecai – *Film adaptations*
                         The Street.
Canadians. Cultural identity
                   Propaganda Message.
Christmas – Stories
                The Story of Christmas.
Cities. Growth – *Satirical treatment*
                        Boomsville.

Appendix

Color
> **Carrousel.**

Colored dancing shapes
> **Hoppity Pop.**

Communities. Change. Citizen involvement
> **Citizen Harold.**

Death. Reactions of families – *Stories*
> **The Street.**

Doodles – *Humorous treatment*
> **Doodle Film.**

Energy
> **Energy and Matter.**

Energy. Conservation – *Humorous treatment*
> **The Energy Carol.**

Environment. Pollution
> **Paradise Lost.**

Fire. Origin
> **Hot Stuff.**

Flying. Attempts by man
> **Icarus.**

Frogs – *Stories*
> **Mr. Frog Went A-Courting.**

Ghanaian folk tales. Special themes: Friendship
> **Ananse's Farm.**

Indian legends. Special subjects: Death
> **How Death Came to Earth.**

Individuality – *Satirical treatment*
> **The House that Jack Built.**

Interpersonal relationships
> **Neighbours.**
> **Spinnolio.**
> **Under the Rainbow.**

Man. Conformity – *Satirical treatment*
> **The House that Jack Built.**

Man. Reproduction
> **About Puberty and Reproduction.**

Man. Self-Image – *Humorous treatment*
> **The House that Jack Built.**

Matter
> **Energy and Matter.**

Mice – *Stories*
> **Mr. Frog Went A-Courting.**

Outer space. Plasmas
> **Fields of Space.**

Peace *compared with* war
> **Neighbours.**

Popular music – *Film interpretations*
> **Street Musique.**

Primary colors. Introduction – *Animated films – Children's films*
> **The Little Men of Chromagnon.**

Puberty
> **About Puberty and Reproduction.**

Québec. Violin playing. Monsieur Pointu
> **Monsieur Pointu.**

Rescue operations – *Humorous treatment – Stories*
> **The Family that Dwelt Apart.**

Russian dancing dolls
> **Matrioska.**

Size – *Comparative studies*
> **Cosmic Zoom.**

Social identity – *Satirical treatment*
> **The House that Jack Built.**

Social status – *Satirical treatment*
> **The House that Jack Built.**

Society. Role of citizens
> **Spinnolio.**

Society – *Study examples: Cruise ships*
> **The Cruise.**

Solar system
> **Satellites of the Sun.**

Squares: Squares forming mosaics
> **Mosaic.**

Starvation – *Computer animated films*
> **Hunger.**

Table manners – *Humorous treatment*
    Lady Fishbourne's Complete Guide to Better Table Manners.
Tobogganing – *Humorous treatment*
    The Ride.
Triangles
    Notes on a Triangle.
Universe. Place of man –
Allegories
    Zikkaron.
Violence
    Balablok.
    Neighbours.
Walking
    Walking.

ARCHITECTURE
to 1954
    A is for Architecture.

ARCTIC OCEAN
Resolute Bay. Underwater research stations. Placement. Role of deep-sea diving
    Sub-Igloo.

ASTRONOMY
RELATED TERMS
SOLAR SYSTEM

ATLANTIC PROVINCES
RELATED TERMS
NOVA SCOTIA

AUTUMN
SEARCH UNDER
FALL

AVIATION
RELATED TERMS
GLIDING

BALLET
Classical ballet. Pas-de-deux adagio – *Experimental films*
    Ballet Adagio.
– *Experimental films*
    Pas de deux.

BANFF NATIONAL PARK. Alberta
Bighorn Sheep. Life cycle
    Bighorn

BEADS
– *Animated films*
    Bead Game.

BEAVERS
– *Children's films*
    Beaver Dam.

BEHAVIOR
RELATED TERMS
VIOLENCE

BEHAVIOR. Man
Characteristics: Caution – *Experimental films*
    To See or Not to See.

BELL, ALEXANDER GRAHAM
Invention of telephones – *Biographies*
    For You, Mr. Bell.

BIGHORN SHEEP. Banff National Park & Jasper National Park. Alberta
Life cycle
    Bighorn.

BIOGRAPHIES
Canada. Aircraft. Flying. James, Blake
    Blake.
Canada. Alpine skiing. Murray, Dave
    Descent.

Appendix   123

BIRDS
RELATED TERMS
BLUEJAYS

BIRDS
Feathers – *Children films – Animated films*
Fine Feathers.

BIRNEY, EARLE. Canadian poetry in English
– Film adaptations
Espolio.

BLOCKS
Building blocks – *Children's films – Animated films*
Tchou-tchou.

BLUEJAYS
Characteristics: Greed – *Children's films – Animated films*
The Hoarder.

BOYS
Interpersonal relationships – *Stories – Children's films*
The Huntsman.

BRITISH COLUMBIA
Mountainous regions. Forests. Fires
Small Smoke at Blaze Creek.
Okanagan Valley. Veterinarians
Canaries to Clydesdales.

CANADA
RELATED TERMS
PRAIRIE PROVINCES
WESTERN CANADA

CANADA
Federalism – *Animated films*
Propaganda Message.

CANADIAN FICTION IN ENGLISH
RELATED TERMS
CANADIAN SHORT STORIES IN ENGLISH

CANADIAN INDIAN WOMEN
Life styles
Augusta.

CANADIAN INDIANS
RELATED TERMS
HAIDA INDIANS
MOHAWK

CANADIAN INDIANS
Cultural identity – *Animated Films*
Charley Squash Goes to Town.

CANADIAN INDIANS. Special subjects. Kane, Paul. Canadian paintings
Paul Kane Goes West.

CANADIAN INDIANS. Western Canada
Views on exploration & settlement
The Ballad of Crowfoot.

CANADIAN NATIVE PEOPLES
RELATED TERMS
CANADIAN INDIANS

CANADIAN NATIVE WOMEN
RELATED TERMS
CANADIAN INDIAN WOMEN

CANADIAN PAINTINGS
Kane, Paul. Special subjects: Canadian Indians
Paul Kane Goes West.
Kurelek, William. Special subjects: Prairie Provinces
Kurelek.

CANADIAN POETRY IN ENGLISH
Birney, Earle – *Film adaptations*
Espolio.

CANADIAN SHORT STORIES IN ENGLISH
Richler, Mordecai – *Film adaptations – Animated films*
The Street.
Stein, David Lewis – *Film adaptations – Children's films*
The Huntsman.

CANADIANS
RELATED TERMS
CANADIAN NATIVE PEOPLES

CANADIANS
Cultural identity – *Animated films*
Propaganda Message.

CARROUSELS
SEARCH UNDER
MERRY-GO-ROUNDS

CARTOON FILMS
SEARCH UNDER
ANIMATED FILMS

CARVING. British Columbia
By Haida Indians
Haida Carver.

CAUTION. Characteristics. Behavior. Man
– *Experimental films*
To See or Not to See.

CHILDREN
RELATED TERMS
BOYS
GIRLS

CHILDREN'S FILMS
Ancient Greek fables. Aesop – *Animated films*
The Lion and the Mouse.
Animals. Movement – *Children's films – Animated films*
The Animal Movie.
Beavers
Beaver Dam.
Birds. Feathers – *Children's films – Animated films*
Fine Feathers.
Bluejays. Characteristics: Greed – *Children's films – Animated films*
The Hoarder.
Boys. Interpersonal relationships – *Stories*
The Huntsman.
Building blocks – *Children's films – Animated films*
Tchou-tchou.
Canadian short stories in English. Stein, David Lewis – *Film adaptations*
The Huntsman.
English language. Alphabets
Alphabet.
Primary colors. Introduction – *Animated films*
The Little Men of Chromagnon.
Raccoons –
Adventure stories
Adventure.

CHILDREN'S STORIES IN ENGLISH
RELATED TERMS
CANADIAN CHILDREN'S STORIES IN ENGLISH

CHRIST
SEARCH UNDER
JESUS CHRIST

CHRISTIAN FESTIVALS
RELATED TERMS
CHRISTMAS

CHRISTMAS
– *Stories – Animated films*
The Story of Christmas.

CITIES
Growth – *Satirical treatment – Animated films*
Boomsville.

CITIZEN INVOLVEMENT. Change.
Communities – *Animated films*
Citizen Harold.

CITIZENS
Role in society – *Animated films*
Spinnolio.

CLASSICAL BALLET
Pas-de-deux adagio –
Experimental films
Ballet Adagio.

COLOR
– *Animated films*
Carrousel.

COLORED DANCING SHAPES
– *Animated films*
Hoppity Pop.

COLORS
Primary colors. Introduction –
Animated films – Children's films
The Little Men of Chromagnon.

COMMUNITIES
Change. Citizen involvement –
Animated films
Citizen Harold.

COMPANIES. Wolfville. Nova Scotia
Mermaid Theatre. Performances
of Micmac Indian legends
Medoonak the Stormmaker.

COMPUTER ANIMATED FILMS
Starvation
Hunger.

CONFORMITY. Man
– *Satirical treatment – Animated films*
The House that Jack Built.

CONSERVATION. Endangered
species. North America
Atonement.

CONSERVATION. Energy
– *Humorous treatment – Animated films*
The Energy Carol.

CONSERVATION. Water resources
Element 3.

CONSTRUCTION. Skyscrapers.
Manhattan. New York *(City)*
By Mohawk, *1960–1969*
High Steel.

CONTINENTAL DRIFT
– *Animated films*
Continental Drift.

CORMIER, PAUL
SEARCH UNDER
MONSIEUR POINTU

CORPORATIONS
SEARCH UNDER
COMPANIES

CRUCIFIXION. Jesus Christ
Compared with social control of dissent
Espolio.

CRUISE SHIPS. *Study examples*
Society – *Study examples: Cruise ships – Animated films*
The Cruise.

CULTURAL IDENTITY. Canadian Indians
– *Animated films*
Charley Squash Goes to Town.

CULTURAL IDENTITY. Canadians
– *Animated films*
Propaganda Message.

CULTURE
Canadian Indian culture
The Ballad of Crowfoot.

CYCLING. Québec
Competitions, *1965*
    60 Cycles.

DANCING
RELATED TERMS
BALLET

DANCING DOLLS
Russian dancing dolls – *Animated films*
    Matrioska.

DANCING SHAPES
Colored dancing shapes – *Animated films*
    Hoppity Pop.

DAWSON. Klondike. Yukon Territory
Gold. Mining, *ca. 1896–1900*
    City of Gold.

DEATH
Reactions of families – *Stories* – *Animated films*
    The Street.

DEATH. Special subjects.
Indian Legends – *Animated Films*
How Death Came to Earth.

DEEP-SEA DIVING. Resolute Bay. Arctic Ocean
Role in placement of underwater research stations
    Sub-Igloo.

DIMENSIONS
RELATED TERMS
PROPORTIONS
SIZE

DISSENT
Social control *compared with* crucifixion of Jesus Christ
    Espolio.

DIVING. Resolute Bay. Arctic Ocean
Deep-sea diving. Role in placement of underwater research stations
    Sub-Igloo.

DOLLS
RELATED TERMS
DANCING DOLLS

DOODLES
– *Humorous treatment* – *Animated films*
    Doodle Film.

DOWNHILL SKIING
SEARCH UNDER
ALPINE SKIING

DRAWINGS
RELATED TERMS
DOODLES

DRESSAGE
    Centaur.

ELDERLY PEOPLE
Views on nursing homes
    Nell and Fred.

ELDERLY WOMEN
Life styles
    Augusta.

EMERGENCY SERVICES
RELATED TERMS
RESCUE OPERATIONS

ENDANGERED SPECIES. North America
Conservation
    Atonement.

ENERGY
– *Animated films*
    Energy and Matter.

Conservation – *Humorous
treatment – Animated films*
    The Energy Carol.

ENGINEERING
RELATED TERMS
  CONSTRUCTION
  MINING

ENGLISH LANGUAGE
RELATED TERMS
  **ENGLISH AS A SECOND
  LANGUAGE**

ENGLISH LANGUAGE
Alphabets – *Children's films*
    Alphabet.

**ENGLISH AS A SECOND
LANGUAGE**
– *Films for teaching*
    The Drylanders.

ENVIRONMENT
Pollution – *Animated films*
    Paradise Lost.

EVOLUTION. Great Lakes
– *Humorous treatment*
    **The Rise and Fall of the Great
    Lakes.**

EXPERIMENTAL FILMS
Ballet
    Pas de deux.
Classical ballet. Pas-de-deux
adagio
    Ballet Adagio.
Jazz. Oscar Peterson Trio
    Begone Dull Care.
Man. Behavior. Characteristics:
Caution
    To See or Not to See.
Merry-go-rounds. Horses
    Carrousel.

EXPLORATION. Gold. Nahanni
River. Northwest Territories
by Faille, Albert
    Nahanni.

EXPLORATION. Western Canada
Views of Canadian Indians
    The Ballad of Crowfoot.

FAIRY TALES
RELATED TERMS
  FOLK TALES

FALL. Canada
    November.

FAMILIES
RELATED TERMS
  MARRIAGE
  MOTHERS

FAMILIES
Reactions to death – *Stories –
Animated films*
    The Street.

FEATHERS. Birds
– *Children's films – Animated films*
    Fine Feathers.

FEATURE FILMS
Western Canada. Settlement by
pioneers – *Historical
perspectives*
    Drylanders.

FEDERALISM. Canada
– *Animated films*
    Propaganda Message.

FEMALE
RELATED TERMS
  WOMEN

Appendix

FILMS
RELATED TERMS
 ANIMATED FILMS
 CHILDREN'S FILMS
 EXPERIMENTAL FILMS
 FEATURE FILMS

FIRE
Origin – *Animated films*
                    Hot Stuff.

FIRES. Forests. Mountainous regions. British Colombia
    Small Smoke at Blaze Creek.

FLYING
Attempts by man – *Animated films*
                    Icarus.

FLYING. Aircraft. Canada
James, Blake – *Biographies*
                    Blake.

FOLK LITERATURE
RELATED TERMS
 FOLK TALES
 LEGENDS

FOLK SONGS
– *Film interpretations*
        I Knew an Old Lady Who Swallowed a Fly.
Scottish folk songs – *Film interpretations*
        Mr. Frog Went A-Courting.

FOLK TALES
Ghanaian folk tales. Special themes: Friendship – *Animated films*
                    Ananse's Farm.

FOLKLORE
RELATED TERMS
 FOLK TALES
 LEGENDS
 MYTHS

FOREIGN LANGUAGES
RELATED TERMS
 ENGLISH AS A SECOND LANGUAGE

FORESTS. Mountainous regions. British Columbia
Fires
    Small Smoke at Blaze Creek.

FREEDOM
                    Blake.

FRIENDSHIP. Special themes. Ghanaian folk tales
– *Animated films*
                    Ananse's Farm.

FROGS
– *Stories – Animated films*
        Mr. Frog Went A-Courting.

GAMES
RELATED TERMS
 HOCKEY

GASES
RELATED TERMS
 PLASMAS

GEOMETRIC SHAPES
RELATED TERMS
 SQUARES
 TRIANGLES

GEOPHYSICAL PROCESSES
RELATED TERMS
 CONTINENTAL DRIFT

GHANAIAN FOLK TALES
Special themes: Friendship – *Animated films*
                    Ananse's Farm.

Appendix 129

GIRLS
Expectations of marriage.
Influence of advertising media
"...and They Lived Happily Ever After".

GLIDING
Flight.

GOLD. Dawson. Klondike. Yukon Territory Mining, *ca 1896-1900*
City of Gold.

GOLD. Nahanni River. Northwest Territories Exploration by Faille, Albert
Nahanni.

GOLD RUSHES. Yukon Territory Klondike Gold Rush.
Reflections of Berton, Pierre
City of Gold.

GOVERNMENT
RELATED TERMS
FEDERALISM

GREAT LAKES
Evolution – *Humorous treatment*
The Rise and Fall of the Great Lakes.
Pollution
The Rise and Fall of the Great Lakes.

GREED. Characteristics. Bluejays
– *Children's films – Animated films*
The Hoarder.

GROWTH. Cities
– *Satirical treatment – Animated films*
Boomsville.

HAIDA INDIANS. Carving. British Columbia
Haida Carver.

HAZARDS
RELATED TERMS
FIRES
POLLUTION

HEALTH FOOD
The Sunny Munchy Crunchy Natural Food Shop.

HOCKEY
National Hockey League. Games, *1967–Highlights*
Blades and Brass.

HORSEMANSHIP
RELATED TERMS
DRESSAGE

HORSES. Merry-go-rounds
– *Experimental films*
Carrousel.

HUMAN BEINGS
SEARCH UNDER
MAN

HUMANS
SEARCH UNDER
MAN

HUNGER
RELATED TERMS
STARVATION

ICARUS. Characters. Ancient Greek myths
– *Film adaptations – Animated films*
Icarus.

ICE HOCKEY
SEARCH UNDER
HOCKEY

IDENTITY
RELATED TERMS
CULTURAL IDENTITY

IGLOOS
Construction
> How to Build an Igloo.

IMMUNITY
> Question of Immunity.

INDIAN LEGENDS
Special subjects: Death –
Animated films
> How Death Came to Earth.

INDIANS OF CANADA
SEARCH UNDER
CANADIAN INDIANS

INDIVIDUALITY
– *Satirical treatment – Animated films*
> The House that Jack Built.

INNOVATION
RELATED TERMS
INVENTIONS

INSTITUTIONAL LIFE
RELATED TERMS
PRISON LIFE

INTERPERSONAL RELATIONSHIPS
RELATED TERMS
MARRIAGE

INTERPERSONAL RELATIONSHIPS
– *Animated films*
> Neighbours.
> Spinnolio.
> Under the Rainbow.

– *Stories*
> Bargain Basement.

INTERPERSONAL RELATIONSHIPS. Boys –
Stories – Children's films
> The Huntsman.

INUIT
RELATED TERMS
NETSILIK

INVENTION. Telephones
By Bell, Alexander Graham –
Biographies
> For You, Mr. Bell.

INVENTIONS
Consequences. Responsibility of inventors. Moral aspects
> Espolio.

IONISED GASES
RELATED TERMS
PLASMAS

JAMES, BLAKE. Flying. Aircraft. Canada – *Biographies*
> Blake.

JASPER NATIONAL PARK. Alberta
Bighorn sheep. Life cycle
> Bighorn.

JAYS
RELATED TERMS
BLUEJAYS

JAZZ
Oscar Peterson Trio –
Experimental films
> Begone Dull Care.

JESUS CHRIST
Crucifixion *compared with* social control of dissent
> Espolio.

KANE, PAUL. Canadian paintings
Special subjects: Canadian Indians
> Paul Kane Goes West.

KINSHIP
RELATED TERMS
FAMILIES

KLONDIKE GOLD RUSH. Yukon
  Territory
  Reflections of Berton, Pierre
>> **City of Gold.**

KURELEK, WILLIAM. Canadian
  paintings
  Special subjects: Prairie
  Provinces
>> **Kurelek.**

LANGUAGES
  RELATED TERMS
  ENGLISH LANGUAGE

LEGENDS
  RELATED TERMS
  MYTHS

LEGENDS
  Indian legends. Special subjects:
  Death – *Animated films*
>> **How Death Came to Earth.**

LEGENDS. Nova Scotia
  Micmac Indian legends.
  Performances by Mermaid
  Theatre
>> **Medoonak the Stormmaker.**

LIGHT
  RELATED TERMS
  COLOR

LITERATURE
  RELATED TERMS
  FOLK TALES
  LEGENDS

MALNUTRITION
  RELATED TERMS
  STARVATION

MAN
  Attempts at flying – Animated
  films
>> **Icarus.**

Behavior. Characteristics: Caution
  – *Experimental films*
>> **To See or Not to See.**
  Conformity – *Satirical treatment –
  Animated films*
>> **The House that Jack Built.**
  Place in universe – *Allegories –
  Animated films*
>> **Zikkaron.**
  Reproduction – *Animated films*
>> **About Puberty and
  Reproduction.**
  Self-image – *Humorous treatment
  – Animated films*
>> **The House that Jack Built.**

MANHATTAN. New York *(City)*
  Skyscrapers. Construction by
  Mohawk, *1960–1969*
>> **High Steel.**

MANNERS
  Table manners – *Humorous
  treatment – Animated films*
>> **Lady Fishbourne's Complete
  Guide to Better Table
  Manners.**

MARRIAGE
  Expectations of girls. Influence of
  advertising media
>> **". . . and They Lived Happily
  Ever After".**
  Views of women
>> **". . . and They Lived Happily
  Ever After".**

MASS MEDIA
  RELATED TERMS
  ADVERTISING MEDIA

MATTER
  – *Animated films*
>> **Energy and Matter.**

MEN
  RELATED TERMS
  BOYS

MERMAID THEATRE. Wolfville, Nova Scotia
Performances of Micmac Indian legends
> **Medoonak the Stormmaker.**

MERRY-GO-ROUNDS
Horses – *Experimental films*
> **Carrousel.**

MICE
– *Stories – Animated films*
> **Mr. Frog Went A-Courting.**

MICMAC INDIAN LEGENDS. Nova Scotia
Performances by Mermaid Theatre
> **Medoonak the Stormmaker.**

MINING. Gold. Dawson, Klondike Yukon Territory, ca. 1896–1900
> **City of Gold.**

MOHAWK. Manhattan. New York (City)
Construction of skyscrapers, 1960–1969
> **High Steel.**

MONSIEUR POINTU. Violin playing. Québec
> **Monsieur Pointu.**

MORAL ASPECTS. Inventors. Responsibility for consequences of inventions
> **Espolio.**

MOTHERS
RELATED TERMS
> **WORKING MOTHERS**

MOUNTAINOUS REGIONS. British Columbia
Forests. Fires
> **Small Smoke at Blaze Creek.**

MOUSE
SEARCH UNDER
> **MICE**

MURRAY, DAVE. Alpine skiing. Canada
– *Biographies*
> **Descent.**

MYTHS
RELATED TERMS
> **LEGENDS**

MYTHS
Ancient Greek myths. Characters: Icarus – *Film adaptations* – *Animated films*
> **Icarus.**

NAHANNI RIVER. Northwest Territories
Gold. Exploration by Faille, Albert
> **Nahanni.**

NATIONAL HOCKEY LEAGUE
Games, *1967* – *Highlights*
> **Blades and Brass.**

NATIONAL PARKS
RELATED TERMS
> **BANFF NATIONAL PARK**
> **JASPER NATIONAL PARK**

NATURAL RESOURCES
RELATED TERMS
> **WATER RESOURCES**

NETSILIK. Arctic region. Canada
Social life
> **The Netsilik Eskimo Today.**

NEW YORK (*CITY*)
Manhattan. Skyscrapers. Construction by Mohawk, 1960–1969
> **High Steel.**

NORTH AMERICAN INDIANS
RELATED TERMS
  CANADIAN INDIANS

NORTHERN CANADA
RELATED TERMS
  YUKON TERRITORY

NORTHWEST TERRITORIES
Nahanni River. Gold. Exploration by Faille, Albert
  Nahanni.

NOVA SCOTIA
Micmac Indian legends. Performances by Mermaid Theatre
  Medoonak the Stormmaker.

NURSING HOMES
Views of elderly people
  Nell and Fred.

OKANAGAN VALLEY. British Columbia
Veterinarians
  Canaries to Clydesdales.

OLD PEOPLE
SEARCH UNDER
  ELDERLY PEOPLE

OSCAR PETERSON TRIO. Jazz
– Experimental films
  Begone Dull Care.

OUTER SPACE
Plasmas – *Animated films*
  Fields of Space.

PAINTINGS
RELATED TERMS
  CANADIAN PAINTINGS

PARENTS
RELATED TERMS
  MOTHERS

PAS-DE-DEUX ADAGIO. Classical ballet
– *Experimental films*
  Ballet Adagio.

PEACE
Compared with war – *Animated films*
  Neighbours.

PERFORMING ARTS
RELATED TERMS
  ACTING
  THEATER

PERSONAL RELATIONSHIPS
SEARCH UNDER
  INTERPERSONAL RELATIONSHIPS

PERSONALITY
RELATED TERMS
  CAUTION
  INDIVIDUALITY
  SELF-IMAGE

PHYSICAL PROPERTIES
RELATED TERMS
  COLOR

PHYSICS
RELATED TERMS
  ENERGY
  GEOPHYSICAL PROCESSES

PIONEERS
Settlement of Western Canada – *Historical perspectives* – *Feature films*
  Drylanders.

PLASMAS. Outer Space
– *Animated films*
  Fields of Space.

POLITICS
RELATED TERMS
  GOVERNMENT

POLLUTION. Environment
                          Paradise Lost.

POLLUTION. Great Lakes
     The Rise and Fall of the Great Lakes.

POLYGONS
    RELATED TERMS
    SQUARES
    TRIANGLES

POPULAR MUSIC
    RELATED TERMS
    JAZZ

POPULAR MUSIC
    – Film interpretations – Animated films
                Street Musique.

PRAIRIE PROVINCES
    RELATED TERMS
    ALBERTA

PRAIRIE PROVINCES. Special subjects.
Kurelek, William. Canadian paintings
                          Kurelek.

PRECIOUS METALS
    RELATED TERMS
    GOLD

PRIMARY COLORS
Introduction – Animated films – Children's films
    The Little Men of Chromagnon.

PRIMATES
    RELATED TERMS
    MAN

PRISON LIFE. Canada
    – Animated films
                            Prison.

PSYCHOLOGICAL ASPECTS. War toys
                              Toys.

PSYCHOLOGY
    RELATED TERMS
    BEHAVIOR

PUBERTY
    – Animated films
               About Puberty and Reproduction.

QUÉBEC
Cycling. Competitions, *1965*
                          60 Cycles.

RACCOONS
    – Adventure stories – Children's films
                          Adventures.

RAGTIME MUSIC
    RELATED TERMS
    JAZZ

RECREATION
    RELATED TERMS
    DANCING
    GAMES

RELATIVES, FAMILIES
    SEARCH UNDER
    FAMILIES

RELIGIONS
    RELATED TERMS
    MYTHS

REPRODUCTION. Man
    – Animated films
               About Puberty and Reproduction.

REPRODUCTIVE SYSTEM
    RELATED TERMS
    PUBERTY

Appendix

RESCUE OPERATIONS
– Humorous treatment – Stories –
Animated films
    The Family that Dwelt Apart.

RESEARCH STATIONS. Resolute
Bay. Arctic Ocean
Underwater research stations.
Placement. Role of deep-sea
diving
    Sub-Igloo.

RESIDENTIAL HOMES
RELATED TERMS
  NURSING HOMES

RESOLUTE BAY. Arctic Ocean
Underwater research stations.
Placement. Role of deep-sea
diving
    Sub-Igloo.

RESPONSIBILITY. Inventors
For consequences of inventions.
Moral aspects
    Espolio.

RICHLER, MORDECAI. Canadian
short stories in English
– Film adaptations – Animated
films
    The Street.

RIVER VALLEYS
RELATED TERMS
  OKANAGAN VALLEY

RIVERS
RELATED TERMS
  NAHANNI RIVER

RODENTS
RELATED TERMS
  MICE

RUSSIAN DANCING DOLLS
– Animated films
    Matrioska.

SALVAGE OPERATIONS
RELATED TERMS
  RESCUE OPERATIONS

SCOTTISH FOLK SONGS
– Film interpretations
    Mr. Frog Went A-Courting.

SCULPTURES
RELATED TERMS
  CARVING

SEASONS
RELATED TERMS
  FALL

SELF CONCEPT
SEARCH UNDER
  SELF-IMAGE

SELF-IMAGE. Man
– Humorous treatment – Animated
films
    The House that Jack Built.

SENIOR CITIZENS
SEARCH UNDER
  ELDERLY PEOPLE

SENIOR CITIZENS' HOMES
SEARCH UNDER
  NURSING HOMES

SETTLEMENT. Western Canada
By pioneers – Historical
perspectives – Feature films
    Drylanders.
Views of Canadian Indians
    The Ballad of Crowfoot.

SEXUAL DEVELOPMENT
RELATED TERMS
  PUBERTY

SEXUALITY
RELATED TERMS
  PUBERTY
  REPRODUCTION

136   Appendix

SHAPES
RELATED TERMS
GEOMETRIC SHAPES

SHEEP. Banff National Park & Jasper National Park. Alberta Bighorn sheep. Life cycle
      Bighorn.

SHIPS
RELATED TERMS
CRUISE SHIPS

SHORT STORIES IN ENGLISH
RELATED TERMS
CANADIAN SHORT STORIES IN ENGLISH

SIZE
– *Comparative studies – Animated films*
      Cosmic Zoom.

SKIING, Canada
Alpine skiing. Murray, Dave – *Biographies*
      Descent.

SKYSCRAPERS. Manhattan. New York *(City)*
Construction by Mohawk, 1960–1969
      High Steel.

SLEIGHING
RELATED TERMS
TOBOGGANING

SOARING
SEARCH UNDER
GLIDING

SOCIAL BEHAVIOR
RELATED TERMS
CONFORMITY

SOCIAL CLASSES
RELATED TERMS
SOCIAL STATUS

SOCIAL CONFLICT
RELATED TERMS
VIOLENCE
WAR

SOCIAL CONTROL. Dissent
Compared with crucifixion of Jesus Christ
      Espolio.

SOCIAL IDENTITY
– *Satirical treatment – Animated films*
  The House that Jack Built.

SOCIAL LIFE. Netsilik. Arctic region. Canada
  The Netsilik Eskimo Today.

SOCIAL PSYCHOLOGY
RELATED TERMS
INTERPERSONAL RELATIONSHIPS

SOCIAL STATUS
– *Satirical treatment – Animated films*
  The House that Jack Built.

SOCIETY
RELATED TERMS
COMMUNITIES

SOCIETY
Role of citizens – *Animated films*
      Spinnolio.
– *Study examples: Cruise ships – Animated films*
      The Cruise.

SOLAR SYSTEM
– *Animated films*
    Satellites of the Sun.

Appendix 137

SONGS
RELATED TERMS
FOLK SONGS

SPACE. ASTRONOMY
SEARCH UNDER
OUTER SPACE

SPECIES
RELATED TERMS
ENDANGERED SPECIES

SQUARES
Squares forming mosaics –
Animated films
Mosaic.

STARVATION
– *Computer animated films*
Hunger.
Use for weight reduction –
Feature films
A Matter of Fat.

STATES OF MATTER
RELATED TERMS
PLASMAS

STATUS. SOCIETY
SEARCH UNDER
SOCIAL STATUS

STEIN, DAVID LEWIS. Canadian short stories in English
– *Film adaptations – Children's films*
The Huntsman.

TABLE MANNERS
– *Humorous treatment – Animated films*
Lady Fishbourne's Complete Guide to Better Table Manners.

TALES
RELATED TERMS
FOLK TALES

TECTONICS
RELATED TERMS
CONTINENTAL DRIFT

TELEPHONES
Invention by Bell, Alexander Graham – *Biographies*
For You, Mr. Bell.

THEATER. Wolfville. Nova Scotia Companies: Mermaid Theatre. Performances of Micmac Indian legends
Medoonak the Stormmaker.

THEATRICAL DANCE
RELATED TERMS
BALLET

TIME
RELATED TERMS
SEASONS

TOBOGGANING
– *Humorous treatment – Animated films*
The Ride.

TOWNS
RELATED TERMS
CITIES

TOYS
RELATED TERMS
BLOCKS
WAR TOYS

TRAINING. HORSES
RELATED TERMS
DRESSAGE

TRANSPORTATION
RELATED TERMS
CYCLING
SHIPS

TRIANGLES
– *Animated films*
    Notes on a Triangle.

UNDERWATER DIVING
RELATED TERMS
DEEP-SEA DIVING

UNDERWATER RESEARCH STATIONS. Resolute Bay. Arctic Ocean Placement. Role of deep-sea diving
    Sub-Igloo.

UNITED STATES
RELATED TERMS
NEW YORK (*CITY*)

UNIVERSE
– *Animated films*
    Cosmic Zoom.
Place of man – *Allegories* – *Animated films*
    Zikkaron.

UPLAND REGIONS
RELATED TERMS
MOUNTAINOUS REGIONS

URBAN REGIONS
RELATED TERMS
CITIES

VEGETARIANISM
RELATED TERMS
HEALTH FOOD

VERTEBRATES
RELATED TERMS
BIRDS
FROGS

VETERINARIANS. Okanagan Valley. British Columbia
    Canaries to Clydesdales.

VIOLENCE
– *Animated films*
    Balablok.
    Neighbours.

VIOLIN PLAYING. Québec
Monsieur Pointu – *Animated films*
    Monsieur Pointu.

VISUAL ARTS
RELATED TERMS
ARCHITECTURE

WALKING
– *Animated films*
    Walking.

WAR
Compared with peace – *Animated films*
    Neighbours.

WAR TOYS
Psychological aspects
    Toys.

WATER RESOURCES
Conservation
    Element 3.

WEIGHT
Reduction. Use of starvation – *Feature films*
    A Matter of Fat.

WESTERN CANADA
RELATED TERMS
PRAIRIE PROVINCES

WESTERN CANADA
Exploration & settlement. Views of Canadian Indians
    The Ballad of Crowfoot.
Settlement by pioneers – *Historical perspectives* – *Feature films*
    Drylanders.

WHITE, E.B. American short stories
  – *Film adaptations – Animated films*
    The Family that Dwelt Apart.

WINTER SPORTS
  RELATED TERMS
    HOCKEY
    TOBOGGANING

WOLFVILLE. Nova Scotia
  Theater. Companies: Mermaid Theatre. Performances of Micmac Indian legends
    Medoonak the Stormmaker.

WOMEN
  RELATED TERMS
    GIRLS
    MOTHERS

WOMEN
  Views on marriage
    "...and They Lived Happily Ever After".

WORKING MOTHERS
  Life styles
    Mothers Are People.

WRITING SYSTEMS
  RELATED TERMS
    ALPHABETS

YUKON TERRITORY
  Gold rushes: Klondike Gold Rush. Reflections of Berton, Pierre
    City of Gold.
  Klondike. Dawson. Gold. Mining, ca. 1896–1900
    City of Gold.

Bibliography

Abbott, George, Gerald Brong, James Brown, and Jenny Johnson. "A National Data Base for Audiovisual Resources Project: MEDIA BASE: Working Papers for Discussion Purposes," Pullman, Wash.: 1976. (Typewritten.)

Archival Moving Image Materials: A Cataloging Manual. Washington, D.C.: Library of Congress Cataloging Distribution Service, 1984.

Atherton, Pauline A., and Karen Markey. "Library of Congress Subject Headings in BOOKS. An Indepth Vocabulary Analysis." In *Subject Access Project: Books Are for Use,* 30–36. Final Report to the Council on Library Resources. Syracuse, N.Y.: Syracuse University, School of Information Studies, 1978. ED 156 131.

Austin, Derek. *PRECIS: A Manual of Concept Analysis and Subject Indexing.* London: Council of the British National Library, 1974.

———. "Development of PRECIS: A Theoretical and Technical History," *Journal of Documentation* 30: 47–102 (March 1974).

———. "PRECIS in a Multilingual Context: Part 1, PRECIS: An Overview," *Libri* 26: 1–37 (March 1976).

———. and J. A. Digger. "PRECIS: The Preserved Context Index System," *Library Resources and Technical Services* 21: 13–20 (Winter 1977).

———, and Mary Dykstra. *PRECIS: A Manual of Concept Analysis and Subject Indexing.* 2nd ed. London: British Library, Bibliographic Services Division, 1984.

Barry, John. "Films for Libraries," *Library Journal* 30: 259 (October 1939).

Bates, Marcia J. "Factors Affecting Subject Catalog Search Success," *Journal of the American Society for Information Science* 28: 161–69 (1977a).

———. "System Meets User: Problems in Matching Subject Search Terms," *Information Processing and Management* 13: 367–75 (1977b).

Berman, Sanford, ed. *Cataloging Special Materials: Critiques and Innovations.* Phoenix, Ariz.: Oryx Press, 1986.

———. *Prejudices and Antipathies: A Tract on the Library of Congress Subject Heads (sic) Concerning People.* Metuchen, N.J.: Scarecrow Press, 1971.

Bogar, Constance W. *Annotated Bibliography of Published Literature on the Cataloging and Classification of Films, Pictures, and Slides in Architecture, City Planning, and Art.* Monticello, Ill.: Council of Planning Librarians, 1973.

Bonnici, N. "PRECIS and LCSH in the British Library: Problems of Consistency and Equivalance," *Cataloguing & Indexing* 56: 9–11 (1980).

Bibliography

Brown, James, ed. *Nonprint Media Information Networking: Status and Potentials.* Stanford, Calif.: ERIC Clearinghouse on Information Resources, August 1967. ED 126 857.

Burtis, A. R. "PRECIS: An Alternative to Library of Congress Subject Headings," *New Jersey Libraries* 10: 21–22 (1977).

California Library Association, AV Division, Subject Heading Committee. *Public Library Subject Headings for 16mm Motion Pictures.* Sacramento, Calif.: California Library Association, 1971.

Cataloging Commission, International Federation of Film Archives. *Film Cataloging.* New York: Burt Franklin, 1979.

Chan, Lois Mai. "Alphabetical Arrangement and Subject Collocation in Library of Congress Subject Headings," *Library Resources and Technical Services* 21: 156–69 (1977).

―――. " 'American Poetry' but 'Satire, American': The Direct and Inverted Forms of Subject Headings Containing National Adjectives," *Library Resources and Technical Services* 17: 330–39 (1973).

―――. *Library of Congress Subject Headings: Principles and Applications.* 2nd ed., Littleton, Colo.: Libraries Unlimited, 1986.

―――. "The Period Subdivision in Subject Headings," *Library Resources and Technical Services* 16: 453–59 (1972).

Christ, John M. *Concepts and Subject Headings: Their Relation in Information Retrieval and Library Science.* Metuchen, N.J.: Scarecrow Press, 1972.

Cochrane, Pauline. "Modern Subject Access in the Online Age," *American Libraries* 5: 80–83, 145–50, 250–55, 336–39, 438–42, February–June, 1984.

―――. "Where Do We Go from Here?" *Online Review* 5: 30–42 (July 1981).

―――, and Monika Kirkland. *Critical Views of LCSH: The Library of Congress Subject Headings; A Bibliographic Essay and an Analysis of Vocabulary Control of LCSH.* Syracuse, N.Y.: ERIC Clearinghouse on Information Resources, 1981. ED 208 900.

Committee for the Coordination of National Bibliographic Control. *The Subject Access Problem—Opportunities for Solution: A Workshop.* Springfield, Va., October 18–20, 1978. (Typewritten.)

Cote, Jean-Pierre. "Precis et le Systeme de Vedettes-Matiere de la Library of Congress: Vers une Etude Comparative Globale," *Documentation et Bibliotheques* 14: 11–21 (March 1979).

Cox, Carl T. "The Cataloging of Nonbook Materials, Basic Guidelines," *Library Resources & Technical Services* 15: 472–78 (Fall 1971).

Daily, Jay. "The Grammar of Subject Headings: A Formulation of Rules for Subject Headings Based on a Syntactical and Morphological Analysis of the Library of Congress List." Ph.D. diss. Columbia University, 1957.

Descriptive Terms for Graphic Materials: Genre & Physical Characteristics Headings. Washington, D.C.: LC Cataloging Distribution Service, 1987.

Dykstra, Mary. *Access to Film Information: An Indexing and Retrieval System for The National Film Board of Canada.* Halifax, Nova Scotia: Dalhousie University, 1977.

―――. "LC Subject Headings Disguised as Thesaurus, *Library Journal* 13 no. 4: 42–46 (March 1, 1988).

―――. "Lion That Squeaked: A Plea to the Library of Congress to Adopt the British PRECIS System," *Library Journal* 103: 1570–72 (September 1, 1978).

―――. PRECIS: A Primer. Metuchin, N.J.: Scarecrow Press, 1987.

————, ed. *PRECIS: Current Publications.* Occasional Papers no. 39. Halifax, Nova Scotia: Dalhousie University Libraries and School of Library Service, 1986.

Evensen, Ole Gunnar. *PRECIS-basert Gjenfinningssystem for Kortfilm.* Oslo, Norway: Hovedoppgave ved Statens Bibliotekhogskole, 1980.

Foskett, A. C. *The Subject Approach to Information.* 3rd ed. Hamden, Conn.: Linnet Books, 1977.

Frarey, Carlyle J. "Subject Headings." In *The State of the Library Art,* vol. 1, pt. 2. New Brunswick, N.J.: Rutgers Graduate School of Library Science, 1960.

Frost, Carolyn. *Cataloging Non-Book Materials: Problems in Theory and Practice.* Littleton, Colo.: Libraries Unlimited, 1983.

Fussler, Herman H., and Karl Kocher. "Contemporary Issues in Bibliographic Control," *Library Quarterly* 47: 241 (July 1977).

Genre Terms: A Thesaurus for Use in Rare Book and Special Collections Cataloging. Chicago: Association of College and Research Libraries, 1983.

Godman, H. J. A. *The Development of National and International Information Systems and Networks Involving Combinations of Print and Non-Print Media.* Arlington, Va.: ERIC Document Reproduction Service, 1978. ED 168 533.

Gorman, Michael. "How the Machine May Yet Save LCSH," *American Libraries* 11: 557 (October 1980).

Graham, Paul. "Current Developments in Audiovisual Cataloging," *Library Trends* 34, no. 1: 55–66 (Summer 1985).

Graphical Materials: Rules for Describing Original Items & Historical Collections. Washington, D.C.: LC Cataloging Distribution Service, 1982.

Grove, Pearce, and Evelyn Clement, eds. *Bibliographic Control of Nonprint Media.* Chicago: American Library Association, 1972.

Harris, Jessica Lee. *Subject Analysis: Computer Implications of Rigorous Definition.* Metuchen, N.J.: Scarecrow Press, 1970.

————. "Subject Headings: Factors Influencing Formation and Choice, with Specific Reference to Library of Congress and H. W. Wilson Practice," Ph.D. diss., Columbia University, 1969. In *Dissertation Abstracts International* 30 (1970).

Haykin, David Judson. *Project for a Subject Heading Code: Revised.* Washington, D.C.: U.S. Government Printing Office, 1957.

————. *Subject Headings: A Practical Guide.* Washington, D.C.: U.S. Government Printing Office, 1951.

Hennepin County Library 1979 16mm Film Catalog. Hennepin County, Minn.: Hennepin County Library, 1979.

Hennepin County Library, Cataloging Section. *Cataloging Bulletin* no. 1. Edina, Minn.: 1973–.

Hensel, Evelyn. "Treatment of Nonbook Materials," *Library Trends* 2: 187–98 (1953).

Herrick, Doug. "Toward a National Film Collection: Motion Pictures at the Library of Congress," *Film Library Quarterly* 13, no. 2–3: 5–25 (1980).

Holley, Robert, and Robert Kellheffer. "Is There an Answer to the Subject Access Crisis?" *Cataloging and Classification Quarterly* 1 no. 2/3: 124–34 (1982).

Immroth, John Phillip. *Analysis of Vocabulary Control in Library of Congress Classification and Subject Headings.* Research Studies in Library Science 3. Littleton, Colo.: Libraries Unlimited, 1971.

———. "The Problem of Vocabulary Control in Subject Analysis of Materials." Ph.D. diss., University of Pittsburgh, 1970. In *Dissertation Abstracts International*, 31 (1971).

International Federation of Library Associations and Institutions, Working Group of the International Standard Bibliographic Description, ISDB (NBM). *International Standard Bibliographic Description for Non-Book Materials*. London: IFLA, 1977.

Jonassen, David H. "National AV Data Base: A Deficient Knowledge Base," *Bulletin of the American Society for Information Science* 5: 17–18 (February 1979).

Keelan, Mary. "The Making of the Union Catalog of Film and Video in New York's Public Libraries," *The Bookmark* 42, no. 1: 14–25 (Fall 1983).

Lambert, G. "PRECIS in a Multilingual Context, Part 4, The Application of PRECIS in French," *Libri 26: 302–24* (December 1976).

Lancaster, F. W. *Vocabulary Control for Information Retrieval*. Washington, D.C.: Information Resources, 1972.

Leonard, Lawrence. *Inter-indexer Consistency Studies: 1954–1975: A Review of the Literature and Summary of the Results*. Urbana, Ill.: University of Illinois Graduate School of Library Services, 1977.

Library of Congress. *Rules for Descriptive Cataloging in the Library of Congress: Motion Pictures and Filmstrips*. 1st ed. Washington, D.C.: Library of Congress, 1965.

Library of Congress Subject Headings. 12th ed., 3 vols. Washington, D.C.: Library of Congress, 1989.

Library of Congress Thesaurus for Graphic Materials: Topical Terms for Subject Access. Washington, D.C.: LC Cataloging Distribution Service, 1987.

Lilley, Oliver. "Terminology, Form, Specificity, and the Syndetic Structure of Subject Headings for English Literature." Ph.D. diss., Columbia University, 1959.

Maillet, Lucienne. "The Comparative Analysis of Subject and Form Headings of 16mm Films by LC, NICEM, and PRECIS." D.L.S. diss., Columbia University, 1982.

Markey, Karen. *Subject Access to Visual Resources Collections: A Model for Computer Construction of Thematic Catalogs*. Westport, Conn.: Greenwood Press, 1986.

Maron, M. E. "Depth of Indexing," *Journal of the American Society for Information Science* 30: 224–27 (July 1979).

Marshall, Joan K. *On Equal Terms: A Thesaurus for Non-Sexist Indexing and Cataloging*. New York: Neal-Schuman, 1977.

Massonneau, Suzanne. "Developments in the Organization of Audiovisual Materials," *Library Trends* 25: 665–84 (January 1977).

Milstead, Jessica. *Subject Access Systems: Alternatives in Design*. New York: Academic Press, 1984.

Mischo, William H. "LCSH: A Review of the Problems, and Prospects for Improved Subject Access." *Cataloging and Classification Quarterly* 1, no. 2/3: 105–24 (1982).

———. *Library of Congress Subject Headings: A Review of the Problems and Prospects for Improved Subject Access*. Manuscript. Ames, Iowa: Iowa State University Library, 1979.

———. *Technical Report on A Subject Retrieval Function for the Online Union Catalog*. Dublin, Ohio: Online Computer Library Center, 1981.

Moving Image Materials: Genre Terms. Washington, D.C.: LC Cataloging Distribution Service, 1988.

National Commission on Libraries and Information Science. *Problems in Bibliographic Access to Non-Print Materials Project MEDIA BASE: Final Report.* Washington, D.C.: Superintendent of Documents, 1979.

National Union Catalog: Audiovisual Materials. Washington, D.C.: LC Cataloging Distribution Service, 1988. Continues data previously available in book form *Audiovisual Materials,* which ceased publication in 1982. The 1983-87 registers are available. The 1988 index provides access to registers from 1983 to 1988.

"NICEM Subject Headings Additions!!!". *NICEM Newsletter* 1: 1-4 (Spring 1979).

Non-Print Media Information Networking: Status and Potentials. Bethesda, Md.: ERIC Document Reproduction Service, 1976. ED 126 856.

O'Neill, Edward, and Rao Aluri. "Library of Congress Subject Heading Patterns in OCLC Monographic Records," *Library Resources & Technical Services* 25: 63-79 (January/March 1981).

Perrine, Richard H. "Catalog Use Difficulties," *RQ* 7: 169-74 (1968).

Pettee, Julia. *Subject Headings: The History and Theory of the Alphabetic Subject Approach to Books.* New York, N.Y.: Wilson, 1946.

Pettingill, Ada. "Film Subject Cataloging," *Library Journal* 65: 27 (January 1940).

Public Library Association, Audiovisual Committee. *Guidelines for Audiovisual Materials and Services for Public Libraries.* Chicago: American Library Association, 1970.

Rains, Ruth. "Bibliographic Control of Media: One Step Closer," *Library Trends* 27: 83-92 (Summer 1978).

Rehrauer, George. *The Film User's Handbook.* New York: Bowker, 1975.

Richmond, Phyllis. *Introduction to PRECIS for North American Usage.* Littleton, Colo.: Libraries Unlimited, 1981.

Roberts, Don. "If You Want Non-Print Media, Don't Look in the Catalog!", *HCL Cataloging Bulletin* 26: 10-13 (February 1, 1977).

Robinson, Derek. "Indexing the Film Catalogue: With the Comparisons between LC Subject Cataloging and PRECIS Entries." *College Bibliocentre Newsletter* 7: (June 7, 1973).

Rogers, JoAnn. *Non-Print Cataloging for Multimedia Collections. A Guide Based on AACR2.* 2nd ed. Littleton, Colo.: Libraries Unlimited, 1987.

Rufsvold, Margaret, and Carolyn Guss. "Software: Bibliographic Control and the NICEM Indexes," *School Libraries* 20: 17 (Winter 1971).

"Rules for Cataloging Audio-Visual Materials at Hennepin County Library," *The Unabashed Librarian* 7: 6-9 (Spring 1973).

Russell, Keith, comp. and ed. *Subject Access: Report of a Meeting Sponsored by the Council on Library Resources.* Washington, D.C.: Council on Library Resources, 1982.

Schabas, Anne. "A Comparative Evaluation of the Retrieval Effectiveness of Titles, Library of Congress Subject Headings and PRECIS Strings for Computer Searching of UKMARC Data." Ph.D. diss., University College London, 1979.

Sinkankas, George M. *Study in the Syndetic Structure of the Library of Congress List of Subject Headings.* Pittsburgh Studies in Library and Information Science 2. Pittsburgh, Penn.: University of Pittsburgh Graduate School of Library and Information Sciences, 1972.

Sive, Mary. "PRECIS—A Better Way to Index Films," *Sightlines* 13: 14 (Winter 1979-80).

Slusser, Margaret. "NICEM, The Non-Print Database," *Database* 3: 34 (September 1980).

Sorensen, Jutta, ed. *A Bibliography of PRECIS.* Copenhagen: Royal School of Librarianship, 1979.

──────, and Derek Austin. "PRECIS in a Multilingual Context, Part 2, A Linguistic and Logical Explanation of the Syntax," *Libri* 26: 108–39 (June 1976).

──────. "PRECIS in a Multilingual Context, Part 3, Multilingual Experiment, Proposed Codes, and Procedures for the Germanic Languages," *Libri* 26: 181–215 (September 1976).

"Subject Headings: Changes and Innovations [Hennepin County, Minn., Library]," *The Unabashed Librarian* 7:10 (Spring 1973).

Svenonius, Elaine, and Helen F. Schmierer. "Current Issues in the Subject Control of Information," *Library Quarterly* 47: 347–69 (July 1970).

Tauber, Maurice F., ed. *The Subject Analysis of Library Materials.* Papers presented at an institute, June 24–28, 1952. New York: Columbia University School of Library Science, 1953.

Tillim, Alma, and William Quinly. *Standards for Cataloging Nonprint Materials.* 4th ed. Washington, D.C.: Association for Educational Communication and Technology, 1976.

Vatican Library. *Rules for the Catalog of Printed Books.* Trans. from the 2nd. Italian ed. by T. J. Shanahan et al., ed. by W. E. Wright. Chicago: American Library Association, 1948.

Weihs, Jean Riddle. "Problems of Subject Analysis for Audio/Visual Materials in Canadian Libraries," *Canadian Library Journal* 33: 455 (October 1976).

──────. "Workshop Papers: Problems of Subject Analysis for Audio Visual Materials in Canadian Libraries," *Canadian Library Journal* 33: 454 (October 1976).

──────, Shirley Lewis, and Janet McDonald. *Non-Book Materials: The Organization of Integrated Collections.* 2nd ed. Ottawa, Canada: Canadian Library Association, 1979.

Weintraub, D. Kathryn. "An Extended Review of PRECIS," *Library Resources & Technical Services* 23: 101–15 (Spring 1979).

Wellisch, H. H. "Poland Is Not Yet Defeated; Or, Should Catalogers Rewrite History?; With a Discourse on When Is an Island Not an Island?" Revised Instructions of the Library of Congress on Indirect Subdivision of Topical Headings. *Library Resources & Technical Services* 22: 158–67 (1978).

──────, ed. *The PRECIS Index System, Principles, Applications and Prospects: Proceedings of the International PRECIS Workshop.* College Park, Md.: University of Maryland, 1976.

──────. *Subject Retrieval in the Seventies: New Directions.* Westport, Conn.: Greenwood Press, 1972.

Williams, James G., Martha L. Manheimer, and Jay E. Daily, eds. *Classified Library of Congress Subject Headings.* Books in Library and Information Science 1–2. New York, N.Y.: Dekker, 1972.

Wilson, Patrick. "The End of Specificity," *Library Resources & Technical Services* 23: 116–21 (Spring 1979).

Lucienne Maillet is a professor of library and information science in the Palmer School of Library and Information Science at Long Island University, where she served as dean from 1984 to 1990. She received her MLS from Catholic University and her doctorate in library science from Columbia University, where her dissertation was on comparative analysis of subject and form headings of 16mm films by LC, NICEM, and PRECIS. Maillet is a member of ALA, ASIS, ALISE, SLA, and Beta Phi Mu, the international honor society in library science.